LIGHT RAIL TRANSIT
on the WEST COAST

HARRE W. DEMORO
JOHN N. HARDER
Cartography • **WAYNE HOM**

Quadrant Press • New York

Acknowledgements

This work could not have been completed without the assistance of a number of industry professionals and historians. We are especially indebted to former Senator James R. Mills and Santa Clara County Supervisor Rod Diridon; Tom Matoff, former Portland light rail startup manager and currently Santa Clara County Transportation Agency deputy general manager for rail; Cameron Beach, Sacramento Regional Transit Agency light rail manager; William Stead, San Francisco Municipal Railway general manager; Michael Voris, bus procurement supervisor of the Municipality of Metropolitan Seattle; Robert J. Halperin, director of market development, urban transit equipment, for Bombardier Corp's mass transit division; A. Weiskopf, Duewag Corp.; and Seymour Kashin, a consultant and adjunct professor of transportation, Polytechnic University, Brooklyn, N.Y.

Jerome C. Premo and Rick Richmond, both former executive directors of the Los Angeles County Transportation Commission and now with the State of New Jersey, were helpful, and we are indebted to Dr. Donald Kaplan of Berkeley for his excellent photographs which added much to this volumne.

Also, Phil Colombo, Portland Tri-County Metropolitan Transportation District (Tri-Met) public information officer; Ann Reeves, Los Angeles Country Transportation Commission information officer; Judy Leitner, public information manager, San Diego Metropolitan Transit Development Board; Heather M. Kunz, marketing and communications assistant, San Diego MTDB; Jamie Levin, Alan Siegel, Nicolas Finck and Robert Callwell, information officers for the Municipal Railway of San Francisco; Carmen Magana, San Francisco Muni photographer; Walter Stringer of San Diego MTDB; and Bill Hunt and Harry A. Bricker of Portland Tri-Met.

Other contributors include Jo B. Murray, Ted Wurm, William D. Middleton, John Labbe, Vernon J. Sappers, Christopher Pagni, Sharon Harder, H. Eric Borgwardt, the late Waldemar Sievers, the late Ralph W. Demoro. Curtis E. Green and John M. Woods, retired Municipal Railway general managers involved in the light rail construction, also were helpful.

We are especially indebted to master cartographer Wayne Hom of Seattle for the excellent maps and to Edward Epstein of the *San Francisco Chronicle* for his advice on the manuscript.

And finally, we acknowledge the assistance and enthusiasm of Leon (Bill) Dorais, who died at the age of 76 as this volume was being completed. Bill was a gifted broadcast news reporter who never missed a chance on the air to urge that the San Francisco streetcar system be saved and improved. He had a second career as a member of the city's transit team assigned to get Muni Metro in business. This volume is for Bill.

HARRE W. DEMORO   **JOHN N. HARDER**

FRONT COVER:
San Jose's light rail line runs in a mall through the downtown and pauses under the trees at historic St. James Park on its way to the north end of the line.
REAR COVER:
Top: The Sacramento light rail line rolls through shady streets in California's capital city, where the summer temperature often exceeds 100 degrees.
Bottom: In Portland, the cars pause at the Pioneer Square station in the center of downtown. The pavement installed for the light rail line is evident in this view on opening weekend in September 1986.
COVER PHOTOS by John N. Harder.
INSIDE FRONT COVER:
Portland MAX 104, by John Harder, Muni Metro 1224, San Jose yard, San Diego 1008, by Harre W. Demoro.
PAGE OPPOSITE: On the official opening day of the Muni Metro system, new articulated Boeing Vertol cars on the N-Judah line pass at the eastern portal of the Sunset Tunnel, opened in 1928, and now entering the light rail era on February 18, 1980. Harre W. Demoro photo.

Table of Contents

JOHN N. HARDER

The first all new light rail system in North America opened in Edmonton in 1978, using German-built Siemens-Duewag rail cars that would soon be acquired in the 1980s for new lines built in the California cities of San Diego and Sacramento and, in modified form, for the rebuilt South Hills operation in Pittsburgh, Pa.

The Return of the Streetcar

In less than a decade, five new light rail transit systems have opened on the West Coast of the United States. Since February 18, 1980, when the first Boeing Vertol cars began running through San Francisco's new Market Street subway and on reconstructed surface lines in residential neighborhoods, brand new light rail transit systems also have been established in San Diego, Portland, Sacramento and San Jose. In the early 1990's at least one light rail line will open in Los Angeles County. Seattle is building a tunnel for electric buses that is designed for conversion to light rail technology in the 21st. century.

Light rail development is continuing on the West Coast. San Diego has a major extension of its East Line to El Cajon under construction, plans to begin work on the Bayside Line in 1989, and has ordered 41 more cars. A local sales tax increase passed in 1987 will finance additional San Diego lines in the 1990's. In 1988, San Francisco is about to begin construction of the first of four extensions and is evaluating the need for more extensions and cars as well as a new generation of rolling stock.

The light rail operations were all built because of increas-ing automobile traffic congestion in a section of the United States with an international reputation for being wedded to automobiles and freeways. Generally, light rail was selected because it offers much more speed and efficiency than buses, yet is less expensive than high-capacity subway and grade-separated rapid transit systems. Because a light rail line was little more than a modern streetcar in concept, it could be constructed in street medians with grade crossings. It could use standard equipment already on the market and proven to be reliable and economic on systems in European cities, where the technology had been intensely developed after World War II, during the same period that street railways were being junked in North America. Several European cities have built light rail lines as "pre-Metros" with the idea they ultimately could be upgraded to grade-separated rapid transit.

Opportunities for Light Rail

In San Francisco, both rapid transit and light rail were built at the same time. The light rail system evolved from an old streetcar network that survived in the internal combustion era mostly because a then-modern fleet of cars operated through two long tunnels that could not easily accommodate motor or trolley buses.

The City of San Francisco, which owns the Municipal Railway, was given the opportunity to modernize and upgrade the streetcar system because of the construction of the regional Bay Area Rapid Transit District (BART) rail system in the 1960s and 1970s under Market Street, the city's main thoroughfare.

The availability of little used railroad rights of way was a major factor in the development of the San Diego, Portland and Sacramento systems. The Los Angeles-Long Beach line will use all of the off-street right of way of the former Pacific Electric "Red Car" interurban line to Long Beach that was abandoned in 1961.

Light rail efforts in Portland and Sacramento benefited from a changing attitude toward highway financing and were able to shift road money to transit and, in Sacramento's case, also take over partly-completed highway structures.

In Portland, the light rail line (called MAX, for Metropolitan Area Express) was built instead of the proposed Mount Hood Freeway, and a section of the line was built alongside an existing Interstate freeway. Sacramento's Regional Transit built part of its RT Metro light rail line on structures for a freeway that was never completed. Indeed, several station parking lots were built by striping the unused freeway lanes.

Some of San Francisco's light rail improvements will be financed with Interstate Highway System funds that had been earmarked for a waterfront freeway the city refused to approve. In Los Angeles, a light rail line had been planned for the Century Freeway median, but an automated system similar to Vancouver's will be built instead.

The Political Setting

Dramatic changes in California's political climate made it possible to build light rail systems in the automobile-oriented Golden State. The pro-transit attitude that prevailed during the administration of Governor Edmund G. (Jerry) Brown Jr. (1975-1983) was a major factor. Brown's anti-highway policies were carried out by Adriana Gianturco, his controversial Director of the California Department of Transportation, who often backed light rail.

Influential Legislative and local government officials also aided in the development of light rail transit. San Diego's system resulted, in large part, from the persistence of then - California State Senator James R. Mills. Santa Clara County Supervisor Rod Diridon was a force behind the San Jose light rail development. A number of elected officials in Los Angeles with considerable political clout backed light rail, including County Supervisor Kenneth Hahn. In Portland, then-Mayor Neil Goldschmidt (later U.S. Secretary of Transportation, and, Oregon governor in

1988) was instrumental in gaining a consensus of local leaders to build the Portland line and played a key role in obtaining federal planning and construction grants.

Aside from the San Francisco Muni Metro, which exists mostly because of BART, the West Coast light rail renaissance began in San Diego. Had the initial San Diego line stumbled or failed, it seems unlikely that systems would have been built in Sacramento, San Jose and Portland, or be under construction in Los Angeles. Without the innovative financing methods developed by Senator Mills when he was in the California Legislature, the San Diego line might not have been built.

Mills, a Democrat from San Diego, came to the state legislature in 1961 at a historic point in California political history. The structure was rapidly changing from a rural-oriented government to one more representative of the rapidly urbanizing regions of California. Mills served in the lower house, or Assembly, from 1961-66, then was elected to the Senate, where he served until 1982. Mills quickly ascended to power during the years when Jesse Unruh, as speaker of the Assembly, was transforming the California Legislature into a full-time body with a professional staff. He served during the terms of three influential governors, Edmund G. (Pat) Brown, Ronald Reagan and Jerry Brown. Mills served as chairman of the rules committees and party caucuses in both houses, and as the President Pro Tempore of the Senate from 1971 to 1980. For a while Mills also was Chairman of the Amtrak Board of Directors.

Legislative Moves

In 1970, Mills introduced a state constitutional amendment to allow some state highway funds to be used to build transit guideways (rail lines.) The measure was defeated largely because of opposition by oil companies and construction contractors. With that funding source blocked, Mills pushed a bill through the Legislature in 1971 that, through a complicated process, established a state transit sales tax fund. The tax plan was a major success and soon became the largest transit revenue source in the United States, except for Federal programs. By 1988, the tax was raising $300 million annually for California transit systems.

Mills did not give up on the idea of diverting some state highway money to transit guideways. In 1973, with California motorists stunned by the Mideast oil crisis, he laid new legislative plans. Figuring that the oil companies couldn't justify an anti-transit campaign so soon after the gasoline shortage, Mills put his guideway measure on the ballot again in 1974, and it passed easily. Now California had two stable sources of transit finance -- a sales tax and a highway fund. Next, Mills moved to establish a framework for spending the money on rail, or guideway, systems.

In January 1975, Mills drafted transit legislation covering San Diego, Orange and Los Angeles counties. The bill,

Boston used the same Boeing Vertol articulated light rail car for its subway-surface light rail lines as San Francisco. Pittsburgh, right, bought Siemens-Duewag cars that appear similar to the Sacramento light rail car, but have an advanced chopper control system. The Pennsylvania steel city uses the new cars in a new downtown subway and on a rebuilt trolley line that runs south from the city center.

as originally written, automatically allocated a percentage of state highway funds to guideway projects in each of the counties. Due to objections from officials in Orange and Los Angeles counties, those counties were deleted from the bill, leaving only San Diego County.

In its final form, when the bill finally cleared both houses and was signed by Governor Brown, it allocated a percentage of highway funds to San Diego County for guideway development, and required that the money be returned to the highway account if it were not spent in five years. The legislation also mandated that only an off-the-shelf system, one already operating successfully, could be selected. In addition, the legislation established the San Diego Metropolitan Transit Development Board (MTDB) to carry out the project.

Bypassing Federal Rules

One reason the five-year deadline was imposed was to force San Diego to build a system without Federal assistance, which would have required a number of reviews by the Urban Mass Transportation Administration (UMTA) of the U.S. Department of Transportation. In an interview 13 years later, Mills said he was afraid the Federal government would impose so many rules that the system could never be built. "UMTA would waltz us around for 20 years," he said.

The off-the-shelf provision forced the local leadership to build a system that would work well on opening day. "I was convinced light rail was the only way to go," Mills recalled.

Although money was now available, a route was still to be selected. Initially, a line to the north seemed most likely, but when Hurricane Kathleen washed out major sections of the San Diego & Arizona Eastern Railroad in 1976, an ideal route to the south became available. The SD&AE's owner,

the Southern Pacific, announced that it would close the railroad rather than repair it, and put the line up for sale. MTDB bought the line for $18.1 million, found a company to run the freight service, and looked for the off-the-shelf transit technology to convert the San Diego-San Ysidro (Tijuana) section into a 15.9-mile light rail line at a final cost of $122.2 million.

"We went bargain basement all the way. In every case we went cheap. It was a low-cost system," Mills said. And it was a success from the start. Daily ridership increased from 11,000 in 1981 to 22,500 in 1988 on the San Ysidro line, and is still growing.

The Los Angeles Struggle

Unlike San Diego, Los Angeles took an approach that was anything but bargain basement, and met defeat continually at the ballot box. The rail system envisioned by the bus operator, the Southern California Rapid Transit District (RTD), was a vast network of high-speed trains similar to the BART and Washington, D.C., Metro operations.

Although the RTD ran one of the biggest bus systems in the United States, it lacked regional political power and often was unpopular with elected officials. In an effort to coordinate RTD's efforts with the state's huge freeway system in the Los Angeles basin, and to coordinate RTD with numerous small bus systems in the area, the California Legislature created the Los Angeles County Transportation Commission (LACTC) in 1976. The commission was mandated by the Legislature to set priorities and assess financial needs.

It was a huge task. The 11-member commission was composed of all five Los Angeles County supervisors, one member of the Los Angeles City Council, a Long Beach city council member, two members of the League of California Cities, one person representing the 82 other

6

cities in the county, and a private citizen appointed by the Los Angeles Mayor.

In November 1980. Los Angeles County voters approved a half-cent county-wide sales tax increase for transit. The ballot issue, called Proposition A, gave LACTC the responsibility for programing the sales tax revenue for transit improvements and to design a 150-mile rail transit network. The ballot measure also required that 25 percent of the revenue be returned to the individual cities for local transit projects and that 35 percent be allocated for construction of rail transit improvements. For the time being, LACTC allocated the remaining 40 percent to keeping bus fares low.

With rail transit money in hand, LACTC began looking for projects. The local sales tax revenues would never be enough to build the costly and complicated RTD high-speed system. While some of the new sales tax revenues would be allocated to the RTD project (a portion of which was under construction in 1988) its success depended mostly on funds flowing from a Federal program with an uncertain political future, and state revenues.

However, a much simpler system, a light rail line, could be built quickly and at far less cost, an ideal situation since only Proposition A money would be used and no federal funds, which required seemingly endless paperwork and studies before track could be laid.

The right of way for light rail already existed, the former Pacific Electric Railway's Los Angeles-Long Beach interurban line. Crucial to the success of the plan was the fact that the light rail project had a mentor, veteran County Supervisor Hahn, a powerful politician with more constituents than a U.S. Congressman because of the vast size of Los Angeles County. Hahn represented much of the area to be served by the new project.

A lawsuit blocked the sales tax levy until the California Supreme Court ruled in favor of LACTC on April 30, 1982. Once that was resolved, LACTC moved quickly. The commission officially selected the Long Beach line in 1982, bought all 16 miles of the ex-PE line from Southern Pacific on June 16, 1985, and ordered 54 cars in April 1986. The first rail was laid by Los Angeles Mayor Tom Bradley and Long Beach Mayor Ernie Kell on January 11, 1988.

LACTC is not an operating agency and after it completes design and construction efforts, the finished product will be operated by the RTD. Planners expect the Long Beach line will carry 35,000 passengers a day in the early 1990's and 54,000 by the turn of the century.

The Banfield Compromise

Portland's light rail line resulted from opposition to a proposed east-west Interstate Highway System freeway through the Powell Boulevard area. The freeway would have devastated the community and required the demolition of one percent of the city's housing stock. The freeway revolt was brewing as early as 1972, the year Neil Goldschmidt, a liberal Democrat who favored neighborhood preservation and a strong center city economy, was elected Portland's Mayor.

Light rail was not yet on the agenda, but because of the anti-freeway sentiment, Mayor Goldschmidt established within city government a technical staff to evaluate alternates to the freeway, and his efforts were backed by Multnomah County Commissioners Don Clark and Mel Gordon. Governor Tom McCall responded by forming a committee of state and local officials (with Goldschmidt as chairman) to consider alternative approaches. Soon the local Council of Governments was involved.

In 1975, Governor McCall asked the Federal government to permit Portland to substitute a transit line for the proposed Mt. Hood Freeway and the U.S. Department of Transportation approved the request in 1976. However, even at this late date, the effort had been mostly against the freeway and not specifically in favor of light rail.

A state Public Utilities Commission study in 1973 had looked at light rail and the technology was among those listed as alternatives in a 1975 survey of alternatives to the freeway, but it was dropped as being unfeasible in 1976. However, planning continued and light rail surfaced as a possibility in a report by Wilbur Smith & Associates for the Tri-County Metropolitan Transportation District (Tri-Met), the Portland area bus operator that ultimately would run the rail line. Finally, in 1977, light rail was selected, but Federal officials did not approve the project until 1980, when Goldschmidt, then U.S. Secretary of Transportation, had considerable influence in the national government. Ultimately, a number of funding sources were tapped, including money originally earmarked for the unbuilt freeway, and state and federal grants.

Instead of building the new freeway, the existing Interstate 84 (Banfield Freeway) was modernized to handle more traffic. At the same time, the light rail line was built in the Interstate 84 corridor, in some places on trackage laid right next to the rebuilt freeway.

In Sacramento, a similar freeway revolt resulted in construction of the light rail line. However, here a section of an Interstate freeway had already been built (but was not being used), and land had been cleared for additional roadway construction, when the decision was made by local officials to abandon the freeway and build a light rail line.

Much of the grass-roots support came from a citizens committee, the Modern Transit Society, which championed the cause of light rail.

Although the situation in San Francisco was much different because the challenge was to rebuild a worn out system, political leadership was important there, as well. In this case, the Muni Metro light rail system was built because of a regional decision involving dozens of elected and business leaders to back construction of a vast three-county rail rapid transit system, of which an upgraded streetcar

James R. Mills

system for San Francisco was to be an essential part.

When voters in the counties of Alameda, Contra Costa and San Francisco approved a $792 million transit construction bond issue in 1962, there was no promise of Federal or state money. The voters agreed to finance the (then $995.9 million) system with property taxes and bridge tolls which was an astonishing display of regional resolve. (The system ultimately cost about $1.8 billion.)

The Guadalupe Corridor

Political leadership also has been a major factor in Santa Clara County (San Jose) where voters have twice approved local half-cent sales tax increases for light rail, bus improvements, and highway construction. A number of persons and groups have been involved, with County Supervisor Rod Diridon leading the effort, both as a county official and as a member of the Metropolitan Transportation Commission, the regional agency responsible for transportation planning and finance. In the early planning days, the Santa Clara County Manufacturers Group, representing the high tech Silicon Valley industry, and the local newspaper, the *San Jose Mercury News*, were significant backers of light rail. A mix of state, Federal and local funds is being used to finance light rail construction.

The light rail line evolved from several studies in the 1970s but UMTA, refused to approve the project. Congressmen Don Edwards and Norman Mineta broke the logjam with legislation in 1983 that required UMTA to approve the San Jose light rail plan. Finally, in March 1984, the first UMTA grant, for $206 million, was approved. The groundbreaking on March 23, 1984, was more dramatic than expected: The blast of dynamite set off to signal the start also blew the roof off a portable toilet!

For a while, the project moved quickly. During October 1986, the first rail was laid and a $17 million shop and yard completed, and on March 18, 1987, the first car arrived.

A short section of the line opened on December 11, 1987 and additional trackage into downtown San Jose was comp-

leted in mid-1988. However, much of the remaining sections of the Santa Clara County project, the sections that would generate most of the expected ridership totals, have been delayed by a lawsuit against the proposed design for a segment of the Guadalupe Expressway, which is to include the light rail line, and by construction problems. Diridon has said that early ridership forecasts might have been too optimistic. At one time, it was estimated the completed line would carry 40,000 passengers a day, but the latest estimate calls for about 20,000.

The Economic Setting

The strong economy of the U.S. West Coast and the growth rates of its cities and surrounding metropolitan areas also contributed to the need for modern rail transit and led to the construction of the light rail systems. The population and expanding economy made it possible to finance construction of the systems.

With an estimated population of 26.5 million -- more than 10 percent of the population of the United States -- California is the nation's largest state. Economists have determined that if California was an independent country, it would have the world's seventh largest industrial economy. It is significant that the light rail systems are in California's most prosperous urban areas.

The state's economic powerhouse is Los Angeles, California's largest city and the nation's second biggest. The city itself has more than 3.2 million people and more than 12.4 million people live in the Los Angeles area, within a 60-mile radius of downtown. By almost any measure, the Los Angeles metropolitan area is enormous. A study conducted in 1984 by Security Pacific Corporation found that on a per capita basis the area within the 60-mile radius had the seventh largest per capita income in the world. That was greater than all but three states, California, New York and Texas, said Security Pacific.

San Diego is the state's second biggest city, with a population of 1.1 million, making it the seventh largest city in the United States. The population of the San Diego metropolitan area is 2.2 million.

San Francisco, with its busy commercial and retail downtown district and a population of 741,600, is the state's third largest city, and the hub of the nine-county Bay Area, which has a population of 5.6 million.

Another light rail community, San Jose, is California's fourth largest city and has a population of 713,400. San Jose is the hub of high tech Silicon Valley and the largest city in Santa Clara County, which has a population of 1.3 million.

The oil-rich seaport city of Long Beach, the terminal for the light rail line from Los Angeles, is the state's fifth largest city and has a population of almost 392,300. Sacramento, the state capital with a population of 322,000 people, is California's seventh largest city (behind Oakland with 354,200), and is the center of a metropolitan region of 1.3 million people. Besides being important as a government enter, Sacramento benefits from the prosperous Central Valley agricultural economy, one of the strongest in the world.

Although Oregon's economy is not as robust as California's, about 1.3 million people live in the Portland metropolitan area. With a population of 370,000, Portland is Oregon's largest city and the second largest in the Pacific Northwest. (Seattle is the biggest, with about 490,000 people.) Portland is a major railroad and port community.

Light Rail Elsewhere

While U.S. light rail development may seem most active in California and Oregon, systems have been built and old ones improved elsewhere in recent years.

Boston's Massachusetts Bay Transportation Authority upgraded its downtown streetcar subway and surface routes in the 1970s and cooperated with San Francisco in designing and buying a new standard car. Cleveland has rehabilitated its Shaker Heights operation and reequipped it with new cars. Philadelphia's Southeastern Pennsylvania Transportation Authority (SEPTA) has bought new cars for five subway-surface lines and rebuilt two suburban Red Arrow routes, equipping them with modern rolling stock. Pittsburgh has rebuilt one trolley suburban line, constructed a downtown subway, bought a fleet of new light rail cars, and rehabilitated a number of existing streetcars. Buffalo has finished a new light rail line and Newark, N.J., has rehabilitated its light rail subway.

In Canada, the Toronto Transportation Commission has acquired about 250 new streetcars and Edmonton and Calgary have built new light rail systems. In western Canada, Vancouver, B.C., has completed an automated rapid transit system that is completely grade-separated and has driverless cars similar in size to light rail cars. The Vancouver elevated structures were designed to accommodate conventional light rail cars if that should ever prove necessary. Toronto has a line with technology similar to Vancouver's. In Mexico, the transit system in Mexico City is reconstructing an elderly streetcar fleet.

Once light rail builders were past the biggest hurdles of politics and financing, they faced an almost equally frustrating circumstance, the need to find a reliable and economical rail car. This was especially difficult in the early years and San Francisco and Boston were victims of the decline of the electric railway industry in the United States since World War II.

Their dilemma was made worse by the reluctance in the early years of U.S. transit agencies to buy proven cars directly from European and Japanese builders, a move that was discouraged by the ''Buy America'' policies of local and Federal agencies and the Federal government's concern over the balance of payments deficit. The Federal government's interest in shifting some of the nation's aerospace industrial expertise to consumer fields such as transit was another factor, and so was local pride.

Light Rail Car Development

The biggest problem, however, was that light rail technology, which began in the United States in 1887-88 in Richmond, Va., had all but disappeared in its native land. The streetcar had to be rediscovered in the United States and be imported from Western Europe, Japan and Canada. In addition, the politicians and taxpayers had to be assured that light rail was, indeed, modern rather than a warmed-over trolley car.

The electric railway did not disappear overnight in the United States. Although industry leaders did not recognize the early signs of decline, the deterioration began during World War I, and for two reasons: The popularity of the private automobile and rapid inflation that raised the cost of doing business faster than fares could be increased in the prevailing regulatory climate, or savings in labor costs achieved. By the mid-1920's the industry was definitely in trouble and by 1930 bankruptcy seemed inevitable.

With their earnings shrinking each year, many transit operators were unable to replace their aging fleets. As the market for new cars weakened, manufacturers were reluctant to improve their products. By 1930, an estimated 40,000 of the 74,000 U.S. electric street railway cars were 20 or more years old.

At the time, almost all of the U.S. electric railways were privately owned and the companies had $5 billion invested in track, wire, electrical distribution and other assets, including cars. In the fall of 1929, a number of street railway executives met in Atlantic City to discuss the situation. That meeting led to the formation in 1930 of the Electric Railway Presidents' Conference Committee. Its purpose was to design a radically new and modern streetcar that could win back passengers and, not incidentally preserve, and enhance the investment the companies had in their properties.

The ERPCC solicited more than $600,000, a major sum in the Depression years of the 1930's, from railway companies and suppliers to finance a comprehensive research program. Several sample cars were produced and the first 99 production models were delivered in 1936 to Brooklyn & Queens Transit in New York. Demonstrators were also produced at the same time for Pittsburgh and Boston. Between 1936 and 1952, 4,902 streetcars, following a standard specification and designated as the PCC type, were built for U.S., Canadian and Mexican operators. The two principal builders were St. Louis Car Co. and Pullman-Standard. Clark Equipment Co. built one car, and all but one of the Canadian PCC cars were built as shells by St. Louis Car Co. and finished by Canadian Car & Foundry. Almost all of the PCC electrical equipment supplied between 1936 and 1952 came from only two manufacturers, General Electric and Westinghouse Electric Corp. (and Canadian counterparts).

Although there were differences between the PCC components produced by GE and Westinghouse, all of the U.S. and Canadian PCCs followed the same basic approach. Mechanical devices were used to open and close electric circuits which cut resistance in and out. The amount of resistance in the circuit leading to the motors determined the voltage reaching the motors. When the car was braking, the motors were used as generators and the electricity they created went through resistors to slow the car (this is called dynamic braking) to the point where a friction brake took over. The cars also had a magnetic track brake. During acceleration and dynamic braking, the surplus electricity was turned to heat by the resistors. While not all modern light rail cars use mechanical propulsion control, they all have dynamic and magnetic track brakes and some can return electricity to the power system under certain conditions.

Three of the West Coast cities that would build light rail lines also operated PCC cars. The San Diego Electric Railway acquired 28 in 1937 and 1938 and ran them until 1949. Both Los Angeles rail systems bought PCC cars, with Pacific Electric obtaining 30 double-ended standard gauge cars of an unusual design in 1940 that ran in Southern California until 1955. The narrow-gauged Los Angeles Railway and its successor Los Angeles Transit Lines received a total of 165 single-ended cars from 1937 to 1948 that were retired in 1963. San Francisco owned 115 PCCs acquired between 1948 and 1974, but most were obtained second-hand and all were phased out by 1982. San Francisco No. 1040, bought new in 1952 by the city, was historic, because it was the last PCC streetcar to be built in North Anerica, and the last streetcar built in the U.S. for about 25 years.

Between 1940 and 1950, the number of streetcars in the U.S. declined from 26,630 to 5,300. There were only 1,262 in 1970 and 1,061 in 1975. The technically successful PCC streetcar retarded but did not stop the decline of the electric street railway in the United States, although the cars were unusually durable, exceptionally quiet and remarkably agile in traffic on city streets.

An interesting offshoot of the PCC program was the formation of Transit Research Corp., which collected royalties for use of patented items such as springs and wheels developed by the research team. The royalties financed further research and, while the PCC was a standard streetcar available in several basic styles, it was continually refined until the last car was delivered in 1952 to San Francisco. A considerable amount of research also was done by TRC on rapid transit car equipment, and Chicago, Cleveland and Boston bought large fleets of PCC rapid transit cars. The TRC effort ceased about 1960.

European Developments

Although interest in light rail, or streetcar, technology waned in the United States, it was on an upswing in Europe, which was rebuilding its cities after World War II, and emphasizing public transportation instead of automobiles.

While there had been some use of PCC components in Europe through licensing agreements prior to the war, it was not until after 1945 that a major effort was made to adopt the technology, when TRC signed a licensing agreement with La Brugeoise de Constructions et Nicaise et Delcuve of Bruges in Belgium. The firm, later to be known as BN in the United States, soon became a major builder of PCC cars and its research further improved the product.

A second agreement was negotiated in 1947 between TRC and CKD Praha, or Tatra Smichov, in Prague, Czechoslovakia, which would become the largest producers of PCC streetcars, with its market primarily in the Eastern Bloc.

Although the U.S.-based PCC car was successful, it was not what the West German transit industry was seeking. The war-torn nation needed a simple and less expensive car as it hastened to rebuild its ravaged cities. Reconstruction of the tram lines was essential to recovery. The major problem facing transit operators was the obsolete design of the tramcars, many of which were small and operated in sets of motors and trailers. Since each motor and trailer had at least one crewmember, labor costs were high. The first goal was to replace obsolete four-wheel cars with larger four axle cars.

To conserve scarce material the Germans did not adopt the U.S. PCC practice of having one motor per axle. Instead, a monomotor truck was developed that had one large motor driving two axles. This compromise initially resulted in cars that were not as fast as PCC cars, but which often consumed less power. To further reduce the costs, the West Germans looked to articulation, the use of a flexible center section, or hinge, joining two car bodies. Rather than having two four-axle cars coupled together, and requiring a crew person on each, an articulated car rode on six axles, with the center two axles unpowered and had one crew member. The passengers could walk through the articulated joint. Ultimately, articulated cars with three bodies became common.

Another labor saving method adopted on most European systems was self-service fare collection. Rather than riders paying their fare to a motorman or conductor, they bought tickets from a machine or obtained a daily, weekly or monthly pass. Riders were occasionally asked to demonstrate that they had paid and were fined if they could not. Another advantage of this method, which has been adopted in San Diego, Sacramento, San Jose and Portland, and will be used in Los Angeles, is that all car doors can be used for entry and exit, making loading and unloading more rapid.

Articulated joints on rail cars were not a new feature. Some sources indicate that Cleveland, Ohio, had articulated cars as early as the mid-1890's. While not widely adopted in the United States, there were significant numbers of articulated cars in several cities, including Milwaukee, Baltimore and Cleveland. Articulated rapid transit cars were used in New York and Chicago with great success, and several interurbans had them, including The Transport Co. in Milwaukee, the Chicago North Shore & Milwaukee, and the Washington, Baltimore & Annapolis.

On the U.S. West Coast, the Oakland-based Key System built an articulated car in 1932 that was the prototype for 88 two-section articulated units constructed between 1936 and 1939 for service over the San Francisco-Oakland Bay Bridge. The cars ran in California until 1958 and a number of them were sold for further use to a line in Argentina. Portland developed an unusual articulated design around 1914 that used two four-axle cars joined in the center by a compartment containing doors.

The Dominance of Duewag

The West German streetcar and subway car market was dominated after World War II by Waggonfabrik Uerdingen A.G. (commonly called Du Wag, Dusseldorf Waggonfabrik, or Duewag) in Dusseldorf. Duewag developed the most widely used monomotor truck and articulated joint. Many Duewag cars were equipped with electrical equipment made by Siemens A.G., another major West German manufacturer.

As might be expected, rail car development occurred quickly but on a conservative scale in West Germany because of the enormous task of rebuilding the country. There was little standardization of West German streetcars until efforts were made in the mid-1960s by the Standardization of Rail Vehicle Committee of the West German Association of Public Transit, or V.O.V., which published a standard specification in 1969.

By this time, West Germany and several other European nations had gone far beyond urban streetcar line development and were building an upgraded version called "limited tramline," or light rail. To operate on these lines, which often were on their own rights of way but not grade separated, a faster and higher capacity version of the streetcar was required. It was a relatively easy effort to adapt the West German car with articulated joint and monomotor truck to light rail use. Likewise, Belgian-based BN upgraded its PCC-inspired designs for the same purpose and even offered monomotor trucks as an option. Other firms, including Tatra, also built true light rail cars, using components that, by now, had been proven in years of revenue service.

The Standard U.S. LRV

It would be some time, however, before European pro-

DUEWAG

The first U2 type rail cars were built for the Frankfurt subway in 1968 by Duewag and used Siemens control and AEG motors. This car design was to have a profound impact on North American rail development because, in slightly modified form, it appeared in Edmonton, Calgary, San Diego, and Sacramento.

ducts would find a significant market in the United States.

In many cases, the U.S. streetcar systems, many of which never bought PCC cars, were replaced by buses as the cars wore out or the track disintegrated to a condition beyond safe use. But Boston and San Francisco had no choice except to retain some streetcar operation and had to buy new cars.

Boston wanted a car to replace the worn-out PCCs running in its downtown streetcar subway and San Francisco needed a new car for several reasons: Two long streetcar tunnels made bus conversion out of the question and the PCC fleet was in poor condition; and BART was building a new subway under Market Street that had a level for streetcars.

The BART finance plan approved by voters in 1962 called for a two-level subway under the downtown section of Market Street. The upper level would be for Muni cars and the lower level for BART. West of Eighth Street, BART's tunnel would veer south to Mission Street but the streetcars would continue under Market Street in a BART-built and financed subway to the existing two-mile Twin Peaks streetcar tunnel. A portal at Duboce Avenue would permit cars not bound for Twin Peaks Tunnel to exit the new Market Street subway, with cars on the N-Judah line operating a few blocks at street level to the existing mile-long Sunset streetcar tunnel, and J-Church cars using surface tracks to their terminal.

Although the original BART plan called for putting the PCCs in the subway, the concept was soon discarded. After voters in 1966 rejected a plan to abandon the streetcar tracks in residential areas and use the Muni level of the subway for a full rapid transit line, city officials realized they had no choice but to design a streetcar that would function equally well underground and on the surface.

The city turned to Louis T. Klauder & Associates, a Philadelphia railcar designer, for help, and the firm designed a two-compartment articulated streetcar with PCC-type components. Aside from the labor savings, articulated cars could increase the passenger-carrying capacity of the new downtown subway because one car 70 feet or more in length could replace one 46-foot-long PCC car. Klauder's design, however, was not adopted, because when bids were received in July 1971, the lowest, submitted by Rohr Industries Inc., was for $515,000 per car. That was far too high, warned the Federal Urban Mass Transportation Administration, which had agreed to help finance the new San Francisco fleet.

UMTA officials also discouraged Boston from continuing independent efforts to design a new car and opposed a Boston plan to bring a Duewag car to the U.S. for tests and then possibly to buy Duewag cars. Instead, the federal government urged all U.S. and Canadian streetcar operators to develop a joint specification that, initially, could be used for a joint order by San Francisco and Boston. (Klauder was retained by San Francisco to continue work on the car specification and the firm subsequently has been involved with the car specifications for Los Angeles, Sacramento, Portland and San Jose.)

San Francisco and Boston Cars

The federally mandated effort produced the Standard Light Rail Vehicle Specification, which formed the basis for the Boston and San Francisco cars. They were ordered in 1973 from helicopter builder Boeing Vertol, which bid $316,616 per San Francisco car and $293,422 per Boston car. Although ordered together, the cars were not exactly alike.

The 80 Muni cars (the order was soon increased to 100) would have moveable steps for use as high-platform cars in the subway and for low-level loading on the street, and be equipped with cab signals and other safety features necesary for fast operation underground. Boston's 150 cars (later increased to 175) would be air conditioned and have only low-level steps. San Francisco's cars would seat 68 passengers, Boston's 52. Both fleets of cars would have couplers so they could operate in trains.

Muni was unable to take advantage of the generous size of the BART-size tunnels because the car had to have a body narrow enough to operate in the old Boston tunnels. That is why the Muni light rail car was about two inches narrower than most of the PCC cars it replaced, and why the front doors could not be used in the subway. The end of the car was rounded so the body wouldn't hit the side of the Boston tunnels on curves.

The Boeing Vertol car had many European features, including a monomotor truck and articulated joint, but the builder did not adopt the specific components that had been so successful overseas. For example, Boeing Vertol developed its own articulation design to avoid obtaining a license from Duewag, and the joint soon proved troublesome.Rather than adopt a simple and rugged mechanical control system for the car's propulsion system, the federal government urged Boeing Vertol to use a highly sophisticated electronic switch called a chopper. While choppers have worked well on many subway and light rail cars, and trackless trolley buses, the design used in Boston and San Francisco has been viewed as too complicated for the service.

Very little of the car originated in the Boeing plant in Philadelphia. The car body shells and truck frames were built by Tokyu in Japan and the choppers and motors were supplied by Garrett Corp. of Torrance in California. Garrett had supplied the chopper control for the Federal government's State of the Art rapid transit car.

According to a report in 1985 by Klauder, the San Francisco car bodies were leaking and rusting after less than 10 years of service because they were shipped as deck cargo from Japan and then sat outside in Philadelphia awaiting assembly. Many of the Boston cars were never accepted and 31 were resold by Boeing Vertol to San Francisco, after they were retrofitted with cab signals and moveable steps, and the air conditioning was removed.

The cars are quite fast, although they do not accelerate as quickly as the PCCs they replaced. However, the PCC only performed well at low speeds and was intended for operation on city streets with vehicular traffic. The Boeing light rail car reaches 50 miles per hour in 37 seconds, but a PCC could only reach 36 miles per hour in 37 seconds.

The Duewag U2 Design

The light rail car that would have a major impact on West Coast transit was first built by Duewag for the Frankfurt subway. This six-axle car, capable of operating in the underground environment and on surface right-of-way with some grade crossings, was introduced in 1968. Like most Duewag cars, it had monomotor trucks and a mechanical control system with switches cutting resistance in and out for acceleration and dynamic braking being actuated by camshafts, and did not have air-operated appliances. The electrical controls were provided by Siemens and the motors by AEG.

The U2 was just what the city of Edmonton required for its light rail line that opened in 1978. The first 14 cars, assembled in an Edmonton trolley bus garage, formerly a trolley carbarn were initially designated RTE1. Almost identical U2 cars began running in May 1981 in Calgary. It was a simple matter to add a moveable step to meet the specifications for the San Diego version of the U2, which entered service about two months later. Stationary steps were included in the 26 U2A cars built for Sacramento, which were placed in service in 1987. Duewag restyled the front of the car for Sacramento, whose fleet is air conditioned. All North American U2 cars have Siemens motors and mechanical controls, with the controls being actuated by two camshafts.

All but one (No. 101) of Sacramento's cars were completed in Sacramento because of federal requirements that the cars be 51 percent U.S. content, and the 41 San Diego

U2 type due for delivery by 1990 also will be completed in Sacramento for the same reason. An advanced car with a body similar to Sacramento's but based on a car built for West Germany that is designated type B, has been built with chopper control by Duewag for Pittsburgh. The builder has designated it as type P.

The Portland and San Jose Cars

The 26 Portland articulated cars, which entered service in 1986, were built by a Canadian firm, Bombardier Inc., but are Belgian in origin and concept. The car is a longer version of the 68 six-axle pre-Metro suburban cars developed by BN (Constructiones Ferrovaries et Metalliques, an offshoot of La Brugeoise) for Rio de Janeiro. Eight of these cars were built by BN, with the remainder constructed in Brazil by Cobrasma. Because the Rio carbody had to be designed to work safely on tracks shared with rapid transit trains, it had a high floor which gives the Portland car an unusually open appearance around the coupler.

The Rio car was built with Siemens electrical equipment but the Portland version has Brown Boveri (BBC) components developed in Switzerland. The Portland traction motor is similar to the BBC motor introduced earlier in Cleveland (Shaker Heights) and which has since been adopted for the San Jose car. The BBC mechanical control system supplied to both Portland and San Jose uses mechanical switches, but no camshafts, for acceleration and dynamic braking.

The Portland cars were assembled at Barre, Vt., mostly from components fabricated in Canada, again to assure U.S. content. Initially, Bombardier obtained a license to use BN designs and components, but later gained control of the Belgian firm, by buying 45 percent of the outstanding shares of BN in 1986 and acquiring an additional 30 percent later.

The 50 San Jose cars, which began entering service in 1987, are based on the work by Canada's Urban Transportation Development Corp. (UTDC), which produced Toronto's new streetcars in 1979-80. Two types of Toronto cars resulted from the UTDC effort -- a single-ended, four-axle car with Garrett chopper and motors (with a mono-motor truck) to replace PCC cars, and a two-section, single-ended, six-axle articulated car. The prototype articulated car built in 1983 had monomotor trucks with BBC motors and chopper control similar to the Cleveland-Shaker Heights cars. Toronto's production articulated cars, however, will have four motors.

The articulated San Jose car is a double-ended version of the Toronto prototype car, with significant differences. San Jose's car has an articulation joint built by M.A.N. of West Germany, and BBC electrical equipment similar to the Portland components. San Jose cars 802 and 803 were completed at Thunder Bay, Ontario, but the rest were finally assembled at the former San Jose Steel Co. plant to meet the Federal content requirement. San Jose's trucks were assembled in Sacramento.

The six-axle articulated Los Angeles car under development in 1988 will be 90-feet-long. It is being built in Japan by Sumitomo/Nippon Sharyo and will have BBC motors and chopper control. Because the Los Angeles project is not being financed with federal grants, the Los Angeles cars will be built in Japan and arrive ready-to-run.

All of the light rail cars use a significant amount of rubber in their suspension systems. The Portland suspension system is almost entirely made of rubber but the other cars all have conventional steel springs. In addition, the San Jose and San Francisco cars have air suspension systems and the Los Angeles specifications call for air suspension.

The U.S. Department of Transportation's Test Track at Pueblo, Colorado, was used to evaluate the San Francisco-Boston, Portland and San Jose cars. In each case, significant technical changes or modifications were made after testing at Pueblo.

By turning to overseas manufacturers for rolling stock, U.S. transit operators have been able to place orders for a small number of cars, yet have the advantage of access to production lines that have produced large numbers of cars based on designs that are continually being refined. The disadvantage, however, is that no body of U.S. experience is being built up, which was the case with the PCC Car many years ago. That has been lost.

The Public's Reaction

Since less than 10 miles of the planned 20-mile San Jose system were operational in 1988, and tracks into the more populated neighborhoods won't be in use until after 1990, the system's ability to attract riders cannot be assessed. Because so few of the 50-car San Jose fleet was needed, there has been talk of leasing 21 cars to Sacramento and as many as 10 to Portland. San Jose may not need all 50 of the cars until the mid-1990s.

The San Francisco system is doing much better, carrying more than 130,000 passengers a day, which compares favorably to the 98,000 transported by the old PCC streetcar system. San Diego's two lines are transporting 26,000 riders on a weekday, Portland moves about 20,000, and Sacramento is carrying 13,000 passengers a day. Sacramento, Portland and San Francisco don't have enough cars to acommodate rush hour traffic.

Muni General Manager William Stead said the Muni Metro has a capacity equivalent to a line of buses 18 miles long. "The real thing you can say about light rail in San Francisco," said Stead, "is that we can't get along without it."

Speaking of his own light rail system, James R. Mills said in 1988 that "the only thing that is surprising is the success of it." Mills is now chairman of the San Diego Metropolitan Transit Development Board.

HARRE W. DEMORO

Once San Francisco's light rail cars exit the new downtown subway they follow old streetcar lines that have been upgraded with new overhead wire and substations and, in most cases, new rail. At 24th and Church streets, above, an outbound J car rolls through the Noe Valley neighborhood, following a route opened in 1917 when Mayor James ''Sunny Jim'' Rolph was expanding the city-owned Municipal Railway to compete with the privately owned United Railroads, later the Market Street Railway. Another Rolph-inspired improvement was 4,232-foot-long Sunset Tunnel, below, opened in 1928 to develop the wind-swept sand dunes west of the hills, which are covered with morning fog as a downtown-bound light rail car prepares to enter the tunnel's west bore.

JOHN N. HARDER

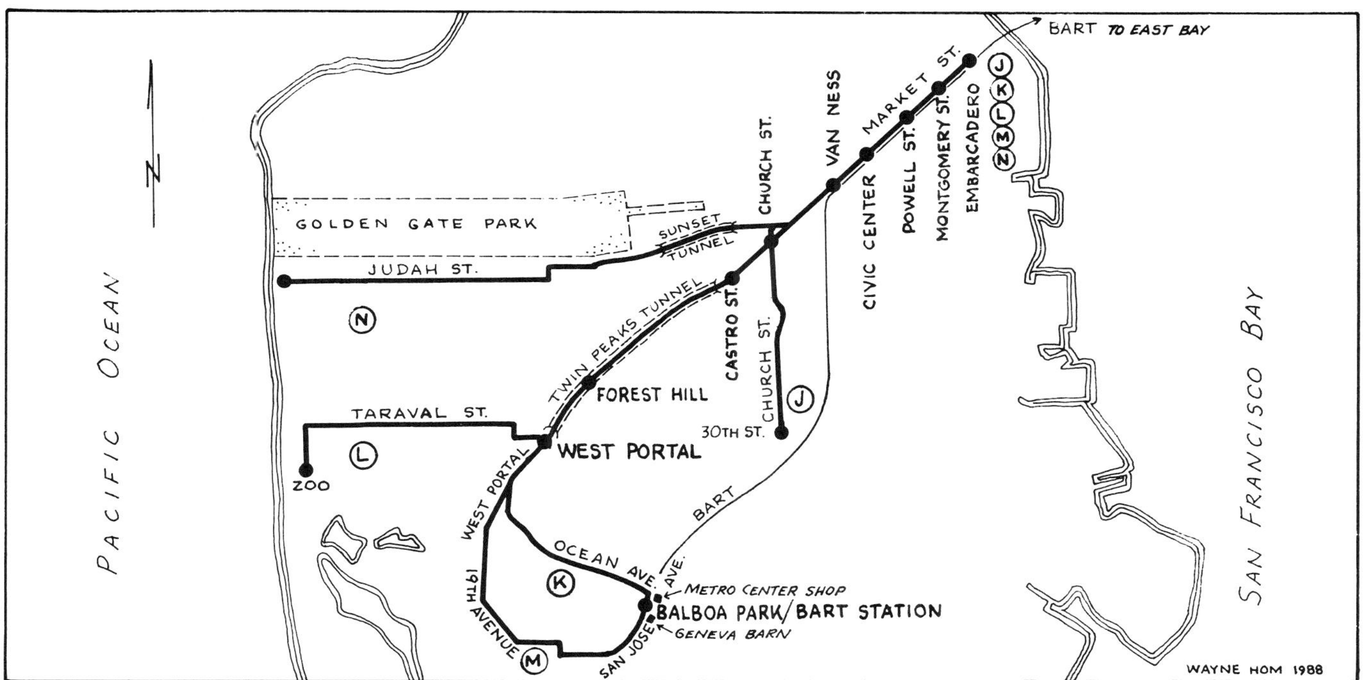

San Francisco

San Francisco's Muni Metro system is operated by the Municipal Railway, a department of the City and County of San Francisco, which also runs 547 diesel buses, 345 trolley buses and 40 cable cars.

The five light rail lines are the survivors of what had once been one of America's major urban electric railway networks. The Muni Metro consists of 72 miles of standard-gauged double track lines, but because the lines overlap there are only 40.8 track miles in the system. More than 130,000 passengers are carried a day.

The oldest line is the J-Church, opened on August 11, 1917. The K-Ingleside line was the first to use the city-built Twin Peaks Tunnel, which opened on February 3, 1918. The second line through the 11,920-foot tunnel was the L-Taraval, which was established on April 12, 1919. The M-Ocean View route opened as a shuttle from the tunnel's West Portal to Broad Street and Plymouth Avenue on October 6, 1925. When the city completed the 4,232-foot Sunset Tunnel on October 21, 1928, the N-Judah line was established. The lines were converted to light rail in stages between February 18, 1980 and November 20, 1982.

The Muni Metro operates underground for about three miles in the Market Street subway between Embarcadero and Castro stations, then through the old Twin Peaks Tunnel to the new West Portal station, and through the existing Sunset Tunnel. In the downtown area, Muni and the Bay Area Rapid Transit system share the Embarcadero, Montgomery, Powell and Civic Center stations. Only Muni uses the Van Ness, Church, Castro, Forest Hill and West Portal stations. The J and N cars return to surface operation at Church Street and the K, L and M at West Portal.

The 600-volt DC trolley system is fed by 12 substations. Catenary is used in tunnels and the subway; there is direct suspension wire elsewhere.

Because of the 50 mile-per-hour speeds in the subway and tunnels and the need to operate frequent service, the subway and both tunnels are protected by cab signals, with three speeds, 10, 27 and 50 miles per hour. The car stops if the motorman disobeys the speed command. The cars are automatically routed through underground junctions. A command center above West Portal station monitors underground sections and power system status.

J and N line cars are coupled into trains and uncoupled at Church Street at the Duboce Portal. At West Portal, K and L cars are coupled or separated. This occurs on K and M lines at St. Francis Circle, the K and M junction.

From 1983 to 1987, historic cars were operated along Market Street on the old surface trackage during the summer. There are a number of rail expansion projects. The Market Street surface tracks will be rebuilt for PCC Car operation to Castro Street and new rail for an extension installed along the north waterfront to Fisherman's Wharf. The ends of the J, K and M lines will be linked, and a new light rail line built from the downtown along the south waterfront to the Southern Pacific commuter train station. These projects have been funded.

Muni Metro is the most urbanized light rail system on the West Coast. The subway section with its platform-loading and turnstile fare collection has the flavor of the big-city subway, especially in rush hour when stations and trains are crowded. Much of the service is stop-and-go. Muni has about 190 car stops, including the subway stations.

Before the Muni Metro was planned, San Francisco was a "streetcar town," and the present light rail system is a continuation of a network that once had almost 1,000 cars but had shrunk to 114 cars and five lines by the late 1970s. The hub of the original system was, above, the three tracked loop at the Ferry Building, where commuters from the East Bay and Marin County funneled into the city before construction of the great bridges. Both "White Front Cars" of the privately owned Market Street Railway and gray city-owned Municipal Railway cars are on the loop in 1939. So heavy was the streetcar traffic the city's main thoroughfare, Market Street, had four tracks, the inside two for the private company, the outside for the municipal system. By 1945, when the scene below was recorded at Powell and Market streets, the private company had been absorbed into the Muni.

16

As late as 1958, old two-man streetcars were still running in San Francisco alongside modern trolley buses and streamlined PCC streetcars. All three types of transit equipment are evident, above, at Powell and Market streets in 1955, 12 years before ground would be broken at this intersection for a rapid transit subway for regional trains and Muni Metro light rail cars. BART had been running in its section of the subway for six years, but work was not finished on the Muni Metro, as an inbound PCC Car, below, paused in 1979 at New Montgomery and Market Streets. With the conversion of most rail lines to electric and motor bus after World War II, Market Street was rebuilt with two tracks and the curb lanes equipped with trolley bus wires.

BOTH/HARRE W. DEMORO

The 11,920-foot-long Twin Peaks Tunnel was the keystone of visionary Mayor James ''Sunny Jim'' Rolph's plan to build a vast Municipal Railway after the great fire of April 18, 1906. The tunnel, finished in 1917 and opened in 1918, was intended as the first phase of the planned Market Street subway, a dream not fulfilled until the coming of BART in the 1970s and Muni Metro in th 1980s. On this page is the original West Portal of the tunnel in 1955 and a scene at the same location with the Muni Metro station under construction in 1978. On the page opposite in 1962 is the tunnel's Forest Hill station, which was upgraded for the Muni Metro. The Castro Street portal, below, in 1968, was demolished for the Castro Station.

The construction of the Muni Metro system was complicated by the requirement that it be built while service continued on the existing streetcar system that the new light rail operation was to replace. Five years before subway operation began, signs began appearing on the streetcars announcing the improvement. The construction seemed to take forever. The picture below, taken in 1970, a decade before Muni Metro opened, shows how streetcars ran on temporary track around subway station work at Powell and Market Streets. On the page opposite, an outbound car runs on a temporary bridge in 1973 over the excavation for the Castro Street station. Below, old and new pass at the Duboce Avenue portal of the new subway at Church Street on February 18, 1980, the official opening day of the light rail system. Only the N-Judah was converted on this date; the J, K, L and M were still using the old PCC cars.

BOTH PAGES/HARRE W. DEMORO

Royal Gate
Vodkahhh 
1017

1140
1140
610·KFRC
N Judah EMBARCADERO STATION
1242

BOTH/HARRE W. DEMORO

HARRE W. DEMORO

The Market Street subway is the main line of the city-wide Municipal Railway system of light rail, trolley bus, motor bus and cable car lines, which carry more than 800,000 riders a day. The downtown subway, opposite page, terminates at Embarcadero station, near the waterfront. This is a three level station, with BART at the bottom, Muni in the center, and fare collection for both systems on the mezzanine level. The Church Street station, used by the K, L and M lines, below, is an example of a Muni-only station that does not have a BART level. On this page is West Portal station built in the side of a hill. Compare the picture below with the views on page 18. West Portal station is where cars from as many as three lines are coupled into one train to run downtown as a unit. Outbound trains are uncoupled in the station.

JOHN N. HARDER

BOTH/HARRE W. DEMORO

Unlike most new light rail lines elsewhere, Muni Metro runs in city street pavement and blends into residential neighborhoods, stopping in front of houses, shops and stores. As it exits the east portal of the Sunset Tunnel at Duboce Avenue and Noe Street, above, the N-Judah line serves the Ralph K. Davies Medical Center on the left. At 15th Avenue and Ulloa Street, below, an inbound L-Taraval car passes a row of typical San Francisco wall-to-wall houses. Like great snakes, two trains on the N-Judah line negotiate the sharp curve in front of the University of California Medical Center at Carl Street and Arguello Avenue. Below, in the early days, cars sometimes needed assistance. In this scene, an inbound car has stalled under the complicated overhead crossing used by pantograph-equipped Metro cars, trolley poles on PCC cars, and the double overhead poles of the 22-Fillmore trolley bus.

N JUDAH
DUBOCE &
CHURCH

Curtis E. Green Metro Center, dedicated in recognition of a retired Muni general manager involved in the light rail project, was built on the site of the Old Elkton streetcar repair shop that in the 1920s and 1930s built new streetcars. A truck from a Boeing Vertol car is in the foreground. The old rail cars were kept under cover but the new equipment is stored in the open, not a problem because snow and ice are almost unknown in the city. Below, against a background of San Francisco ''bay window'' architecture, an inbound N-Judah train loads at Carl and Cole streets in 1988. The graffiti that was plaguing the system at the time is evident on the front of the car.

JOHN N. HARDER

HARRE W. DEMORO

Muni Metro serves three major institutions of higher education. The M-Ocean View line, which speeds along 19th Avenue on a median strip right of way dating from the 1920s, serves San Francisco State University, above, at Holloway Avenue. City College of San Francisco students use the K-Ingleside line, shown below on Ocean Avenue approaching the platforms for the campus at Phelan Avenue. The University of California Medical Center (page 25) is on the N-Judah line.

The Boeing Vertol Standard Light Rail Vehicle (SLRV) built on a joint order for Boston and San Francisco was the first streetcar manufactured in North America since the San Francisco Municipal Railway acquired 25 PCC cars (1016-1040) from the St. Louis Car Co. in 1951-1952. Because of the cool San Francisco climate, air conditioning was not installed on Muni's cars. As these pictures show, moveable upper sash has been installed in some of the side windows to improve ventilation. Note how the plug-style sliding doors retract into the carbody when closed. The couplers were made by New York Air Brake Co.

Muni's 600-volt, direct-current, articulated light rail cars were built in Philadelphia by Boeing Vertol on a joint order with Boston's Massachusetts Bay Transportation Authority (MBTA). Muni initially ordered 80 cars, then decided to buy 100, while Boston increased its order from 150 to 175. Ultimately, MBTA rejected some cars and Muni bought 31 cars intended for Boston but rebuilt at Philadelphia for San Francisco. Prototype cars were delivered to San Francisco in October 1977. Muni production cars 1200-1299 were built specifically for the Muni with delivery starting in September 1978. In 1982, a car built as MBTA 3565 was sold instead to Muni and became II 1252, replacing a wrecked San Francisco car. Starting in February 1983, Muni began taking delivery of 1300-1329, which had been intended to be MBTA 3561, 3567, 3571, 3555, 3572-3574, 3570, 3562, 3557, 3569, 3535, 3558, 3556, 3554, 3560, 3559, 3553, 3563, 3564, 3548, 3566, 3545, 3551, 3547, 3541, 3539, 3542, 3549. Due to other accidents, Muni may have switched some 1200 series bodies and renumbered sections. The car bodies built for Muni seat 68; the Boston bodies, 52. The cars have two Garrett 2000768-2 traction motors and Garrett chopper control. The center truck is unpowered. The car body is 71 feet long and the car is 73 feet long over couplers and 8'-10¼'' wide. The car is 11' 6'' high from top of rail to locked down pantograph. The body shells and truck frames were built in Japan by Tokyu and shipped by sea to Philadelphia. The car weighs about 67,000 pounds, has forced air ventilation (not air conditioning), cab signals for operation in the subway, Twin Peaks Tunnel and Sunset Tunnel, and a top speed of 52 miles an hour. The Muni cars accelerate at about 3 mph/sec. (2.8 mph plus or minus 10 percent) and decelerate under normal conditions at 3.5 mph/sec. The center doors have moveable steps which are lowered for street-level operation. Unlike most modern light rail cars, the Muni cars have fareboxes for collection outside the subway, because San Francisco does not use the prepaid honor fare system.

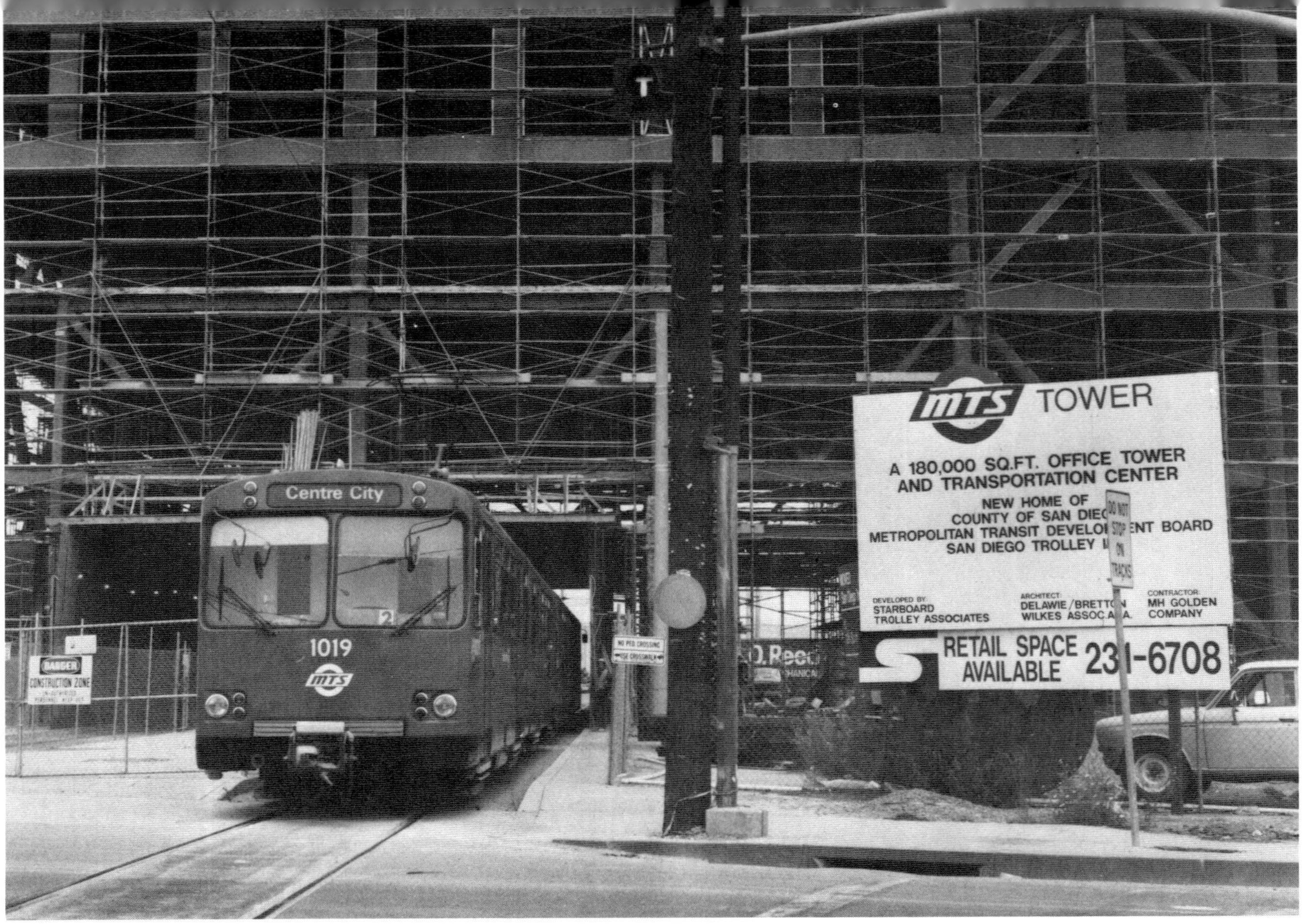

BOTH/HARRE W. DEMORO

Building on the success of its San Ysidro (Tijuana) line opened in 1981, San Diego was laying track to El Cajon and constructing an office building in 1988 above the site of the 12th Street and Imperial Avenue station, which also serves as the junction between the original route and the new Euclid line, which was being extended toward El in 1989. In the morning rush hour, below, a one-car Euclid train, left, pauses at Civic Center station at Sixth and C streets as a two-car train from San Ysidro unloads commuters. Note the sign barring automobiles from the track area.

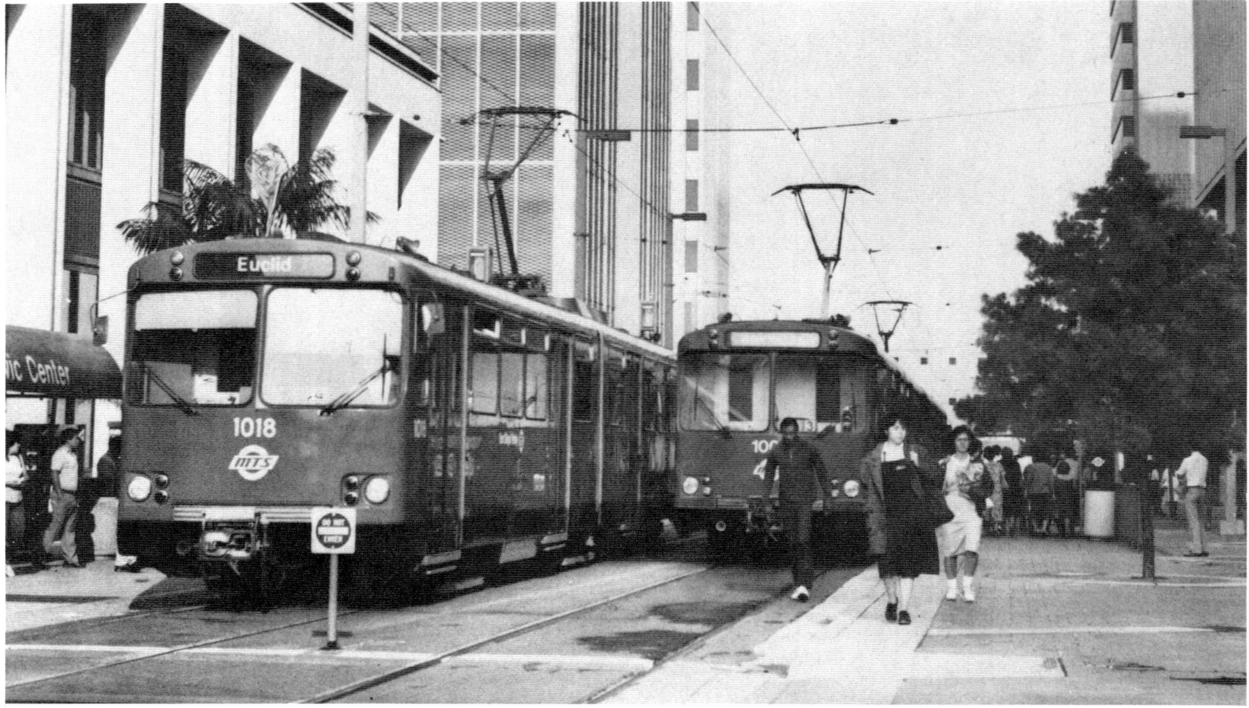

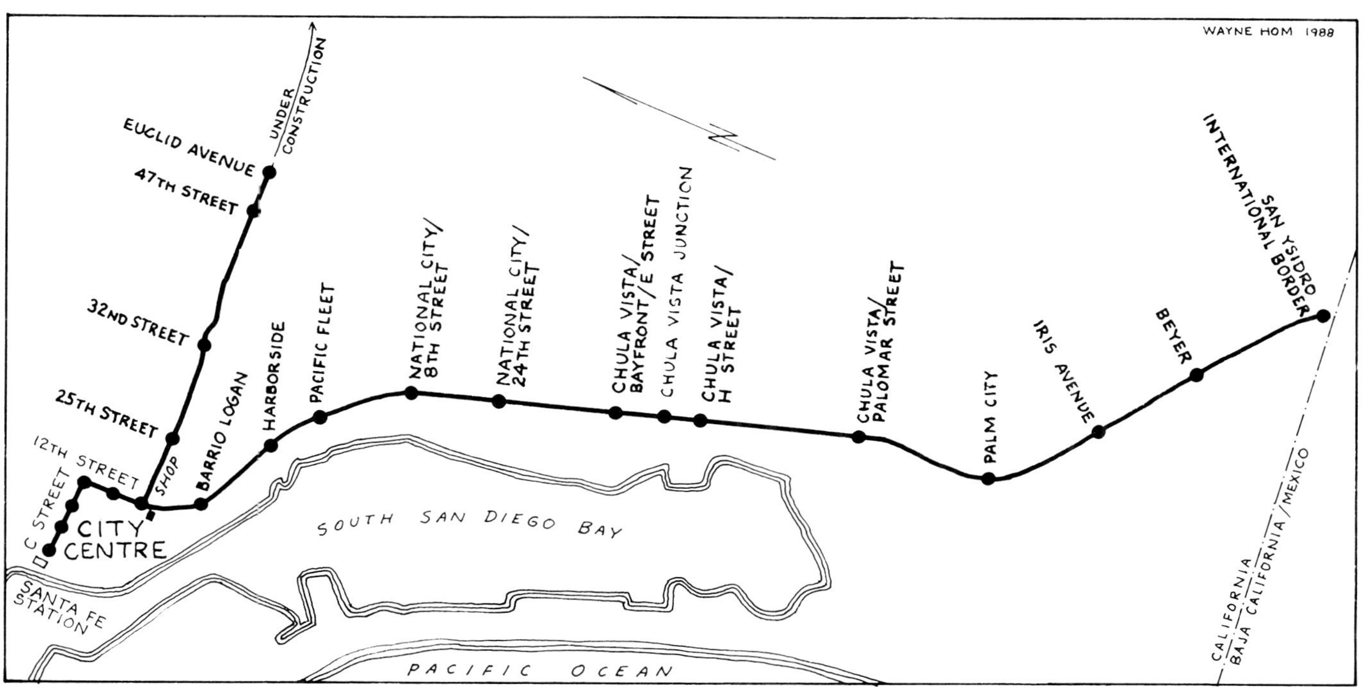

San Diego

The San Diego light rail system is operated by San Diego Trolley Inc., a subsidiary of the Metropolitan Transit Development Board, a public agency. MTDB presides over the Metropolitan Transit System (MTS), a federation of public and private systems operating the two rail lines, 10 regional bus lines, three commuter express bus routes and 37 local bus routes. The rail and bus systems carry more than 120,000 riders a day, with the light rail contributing about 27,000 of the passengers.

MTDB also owns the San Diego & Arizona Eastern Railway, which provides freight service on trolley lines and freight-only trackage. The San Diego & Imperial Valley Railroad operates the freight service under contract to MTDB.

Two light rail lines are in operation: 15.9 miles from downtown to San Ysidro near Tijuana on the Mexican border, opened on July 26, 1981, and 6.2 miles between downtown and Euclid Avenue, opened on March 23, 1986. Due to 1.7 miles of overlapping track shared by both lines, the total system mileage in 1988 is 20.4 miles.

An 11.1-mile extension of the Euclid line to El Cajon is scheduled open in 1989, and other extensions have been authorized that ultimately will create a 112.6-mile system. A $35 million, 10-story office building to be completed in 1989 at the 12th and Imperial avenues station will house MTDB, San Diego Trolley and other governmental agency offices. The 12th and Imperial station is the junction between the San Ysidro and Euclid-El Cajon lines, and also will be the junction with the proposed Bayside light rail line.

The original San Ysidro line installation had 11 substations. Major improvements are being made to the 600-volt DC overhead trolley power system and to the shop and repair yard to accomodate the additional cars and mileage. Beyond the downtown, the lines are built almost entirely on SD&AE rights of way and SD&AE bridges and roadbed were used when possible.

The San Ysidro line was built with a single track but a second track was soon added. The Euclid-El Cajon line has some single track sections. Automatic block signals protect most sections. There is no feature to stop a train passing a red signal. However, special care was taken to install safety devices on industrial spurs used by diesel freight trains to protect the passenger operation. The freight-only tracks are not electrified.

Direct suspension trolley wire is used in the downtown but most of the remaining sections have catenary.

The San Ysidro and Euclid lines share six stations in the center city. In addition, there are 12 stations on the San Ysidro line and four on the Euclid line. The El Cajon extension will add eight stations and tap a major residential area in the Highway 94 corridor.

The San Ysidro line parallels Interstate 5 and serves industrial areas, shipyards and suburban residential neighborhoods. Nicknamed "Tijuana Trolley," the line does a big business carrying tourists and Mexican nationals.

The freight operation is an unusual feature of the San Diego rail system. Most of the activity is at night after passenger operations cease. The MTDB earns a modest profit from freight traffic.

The San Diego Electric Railway was one of the most modern and carefully maintained streetcar systems in the West and in 1937, became the first on the Pacific Coast to order modern PCC streetcars. In its prime, the company was owned by the Spreckels family, which had been involved in the development of the city and took pride in its institutions. In the view above, one of the sleek PCC cars (part of a second order received in 1938 from St. Louis Car Co.) loads on the 2-Broadway line. Below, is the classic mission-revival style station of the Atchison, Topeka & Santa Fe Railway which survives in today's Amtrak era, but without the streetcar loop and the arched entry. The present light rail line terminates on the street along the right side of this picture and the railroad station, now restored, is the terminal for Amtrak's busy Los Angeles-San Diego service.

An example of the interest the Spreckels family had owning and operating a first-rate streetcar that would spur the growth of San Diego was the decision in 1923 to buy 50 lightweight cars from American Car Co. The cars were delivered with pantographs and couplers and could run in trains, and were part of a grand scheme that included completion of a new line to La Jolla in 1924, which ran only until 1940. As shown on this page in the 1940s, car 400-449 had been downgraded, having lost their pantographs, couplers and multiple-unit control for train operation. The Spreckels family sold the streetcar company in 1948 to pro-bus investor Jesse L. Haugh, who abandoned the rail lines the following year. Most of the PCC cars were sold to a line in El Paso, Texas.

JOHN N. HARDER

For the first time in memory in San Diego, streets were being torn up to install streetcar tracks rather than to remove them. This is the scene on C Street at State Street in 1980. Still to come is pavement and overhead wire. Transit officials didn't wait to install numbers and emblems on the cars before testing them in National City. The destination signs read ''Training Car.'' The construction of the San Diego light rail system drew considerable interest in the engineering community and the project was honored in 1982 with a plaque awarded by the American Society of Civil Engineers that is mounted at the San Ysidro station. The light rail line terminates at Kettner Boulevard at the Santa Fe (now Amtrak) station on C Street, page opposite, then rolls along C Street, below, passing an advertisement for racing south of the border.

JOHN N. HARDER

HARRE W. DEMORO

Santa Fe
SANTA FE DEPOT
SAN YSIDRO
1017

AL BANK
RACING EVERY SATURDAY & SUNDAY
CALIENTE!
in Old Mexico
5-10
BETTING DAILY IN MAJOR U.S. HORSE TRACKS
Centre City
1018
NO VEHICLES
nter
OUSE

A grasp of both Spanish and English is useful along 12th Street at Market Street (Martin Luther King Way), where the cars for both San Ysidro and Euclid pass through a neighborhood business district. In the view below, two trains meet at 12th Street and Imperial Avenue in 1987, shortly before the station was closed and relocated to the north to make way for construction of an office building (see page 30). The car with the Euclid sign has just left the yard and will be coupled to a Euclid train. For San Ysidro trains, street running ends near Commercial Street, page opposite, top. The rails in the foreground lead to the car storage yard. Below, a northbound three-car train passes a block signal as it approaches Palomar station on a three-track section that includes a non-electrified freight siding on the left.

San Ysidro
1006

BOTH PAGES/HARRE W. DEMORO

CENTRE CITY
1009
984

The former San Diego & Arizona Eastern north-south freight route to San Ysidro was a logical choice for the light rail line. Roadbed was upgraded and eventually all of the line was double tracked. Much of this track is 50 mile per hour territory for the gleaming Siemens-Duewag model U-2 cars. Pacific Fleet station, above, serves a busy U.S. Naval installation and the station is popular with uniformed personnel and civilian employees. The Bayfront station, below, was added after the San Ysidro line opened and has a third non-electrified track for freight traffic. The freight service is operated by an outside firm under contract to the Metropolitan Transit Development Board, and generates a modest profit for the governmental agency.

Between the Chula Vista/Bayfront and Chula Vista/H Street stations, the San Ysidro line crosses the old Coronado branch of the SD&AE, above, portions of which are still in freight service. The crossing is protected by signals and there is a non-electrified track linking the light rail line with the freight trackage. The train is northbound heading toward Bayfront station. The freight railroad heritage of the San Ysidro operation also is evident, below, in the Golden West Packing Co. warehouse, which is served by a rail siding, just south of the Palm City light rail station. By using an existing freight line and buying standard German-built Siemens-Duewag cars, San Diego quickly built a bargain basement -- and successful -- rail transit line.

BOTH PAGES/HARRE W. DEMORO

Ticket machines, page opposite, are mounted on sidewalks and station platforms, and have instructions in Spanish and English. Tickets, postcards, soft drinks, sandwiches and souvenirs are sold at this stand at the Santa Fe (Amtrak) station stop. The shack-like stand is painted the same red as the light rail cars and the clerks cheerfully explain the trolley line in Spanish and English.

Approaching the San Ysidro terminal, the track parallels a city street; the freight railroad yard and the freight track that crosses the border into Mexico are on the right. The San Ysidro station, below, at the international border, is in a mall in the center of a street. The freight line to Mexico is visible in the side of the hill above the light rail train. The border is to the right out of the picture.

BOTH PAGES/HARRE W. DEMORO

TICKETS
TICKETS
TICKETS   ONE WAY ONLY
UN SENTIDO
CHANGE
Purchase ticket
before boarding
the Trolley.
Compre su boleto
antes de abordar el Trole.

ST.   JERRYS SNACKS
SANDWICHES
SELF
SERVICE
VARIETY
OF
SANDWICHES
ROUND TRIP TICKETS
TO
SAN YSIDRO
MEXICAN BORDER $3.00
Trolley Information
CHILDREN 5 OR UNDER FREE
SENIOR CITIZENS 60 AND OVER 50¢ PER TRIP EACH DIRECTION
"MUST PURCHASE TICKETS AT TICKET MACHINE FOR EACH DIRECTION"
SNACKS • COLD DRINKS
TROLLEY
TICKETS
TO THE
BORDER
ROUND
TRIP
$3.00

HARRE W. DEMORO

The 4.5-mile Euclid line, opened in 1986, is the first part of the 15.6-mile El Cajon line scheduled to open in 1989. The bridge over Interstate 805, below, was not wide enough for two tracks so a guantlet section was built. This involves laying the four rails side by side. This downtown-bound car is entering the special section. In the frame above, a city-bound Euclid car crosses a bridge over Imperial Avenue as it approaches the 32nd and Commercial streets station, and soon will leave private right of way for street running on Commercial Street. Like the San Ysidro line, the Euclid line and the El Cajon extension use an upgraded SD&AE line that retains freight service.

JOHN N. HARDER

HARRE W. DEMORO

San Diego's mild weather that is free of snow and ice makes it possible for the light rail cars to be stored out of doors all year and only a small, two-track shop was necessary for the San Ysidro and Euclid lines. The barn will be enlarged as part of the expansion program that includes the El Cajon extension. The cars are scrubbed frequently, below, with a mechanical washer in the yard outside the shop. About once a year, the cars are hand polished. Graffiti is removed as soon as it is found. The red paint scheme on the cars is an example of how simplicity was designed into the system. Frugal planners saw that it would be far easier to touch up a damaged car if the entire body was painted in one color.

SAN DIEGO MTDB

San Diego has two styles of the Siemens-Duewag type U2 light rail car. The original 24 cars, above, delivered in two batches in 1980 and 1982, were not air conditioned. The third order, below, the six cars acquired for the Euclid line in 1986, have roof-mounted air conditioning units, and the 41 cars (officially, 40 plus one for parts) on order for delivery starting in 1988 also will be air conditioned. Note the buttons on the side of the car that passengers press to open the doors. The car body is steel but the cab end is made of fiberglass.

San Diego was the first U.S. system to adopt the
Siemens-Duewag rail car that was initially developed
for the Frankfurt subway and then adapted for light
rail use in Edmonton, Canada. It also is being used in
Calgary, Canada, and in modified form in Sacramento. Delivery of San Diego's original cars,
numbered 1001-1014, started in November 1980; the
second series, 1015-1024, began arriving in November
1982. The six air-conditioned cars were delivered
starting in January 1986, and are numbered 1025-
1030. Additional cars are on order and will be based on
the design of 1025-1030. The air conditioned car
weighs about 80,000 pounds and the others 71,870
pounds. The first 30 cars were manufactured almost
exclusively in Germany with minor final assembly oc-
curring in San Diego. About 49 percent of the 41 cars
on order in 1988 will be manufactured in Dusseldorf
and the car then will be completed at the Siemens-
Duewag facility in Sacramento where final assembly
was done on Sacramento's Duewag cars. All San Diego
cars have two Siemens type 1KB20213MK02 traction
motors and Siemens cam control. The center truck is
unpowered. The cars are 75.6 feet long over the body
and 79.6 feet over couplers, and are 8.7 feet wide
(measured inside). The cars have folding steps and
folding doors, and standard Duewag monomotor
trucks. Braking is dynamic, magnetic track and disk,
which is spring applied and electrically released. The
64-seat cars are all-electric and have no air appliances.
The maximum speed is 50 miles per hour. Under normal operating conditions, the acceleration and braking
rates are approximately 3 mph/sec. The cars run on
600 volts, direct current, and have Scharfenberg-
Fabeg couplers. San Diego's track gauge is 4' 8½''.

Automatic block signals protect high-speed sections of Portland's MAX (Metropolitan Area Express) light rail line on track along freeways and near the Gresham terminal. As an extra safety precaution, the equipment between the rails in the view above at Gresham City Hall station will stop the car if it passes a red signal. The picture was taken on September 8, 1986, the first day of revenue service. The station at 148th Avenue, below, and photographed the following day, is typical of the line where it runs in the median of East Burnside Street, a major east-west boulevard.

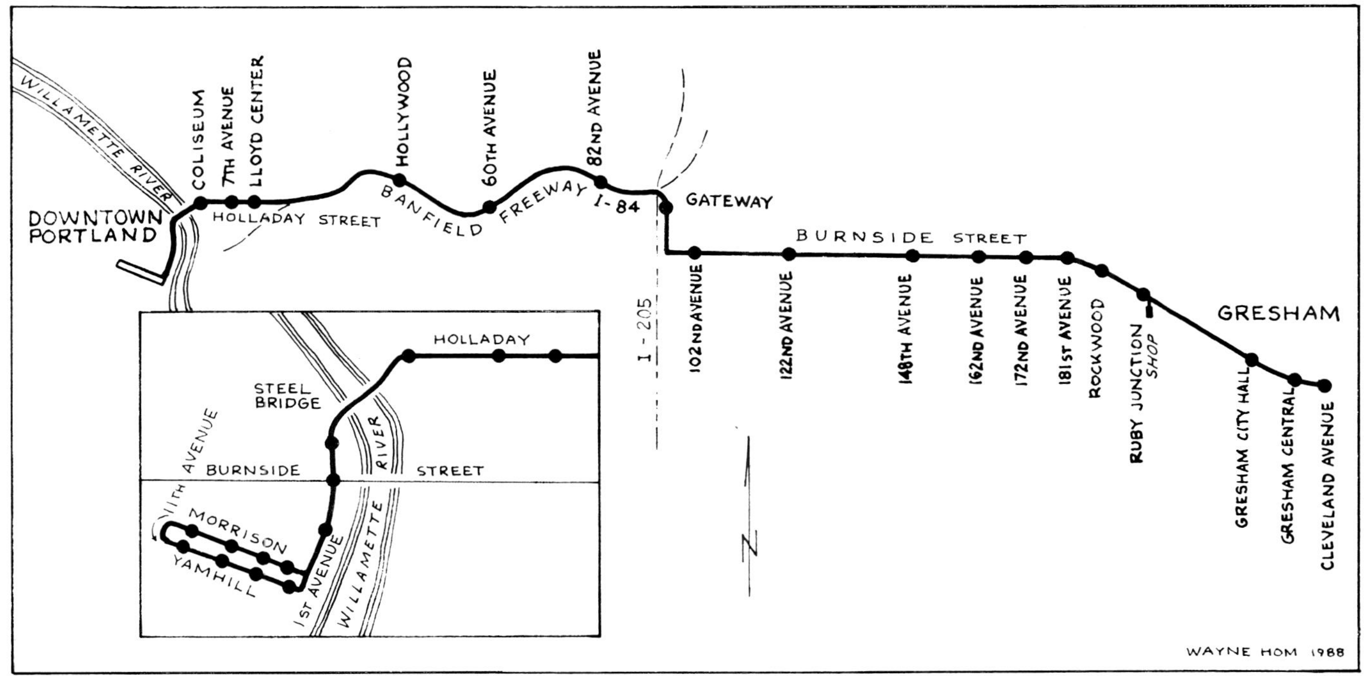

Portland

The 15.2-mile Portland-Gresham light rail line operated by the Tri-County Metropolitan Transportation District of Oregon, also the regional bus operator, was opened to revenue passenger service on September 8, 1986. The line is double track except between Ruby Junction and the Gresham/Cleveland Avenue terminal, which has a long passing track at Gresham/City Hall station.

The system has an ultimate capacity of 40,000 passengers a day and in 1988 was carrying about 20,000 daily riders. With increased parking and more cars, the potential capacity is 60,000 riders a day.

The are 22 stations, each about 200 feet long. The maximum train that can be operated is two cars due to station length and the downtown Portland street pattern. The line has 65 grade crossings. The trolley voltage is 750 volts, DC, energized from 14 stations.

Automatic block signals protect the two high-speed sections, the 5.3-mile portion along the Banfield Freeway and on the 2.5-mile former interurban right of way from Ruby Junction to the Gresham/Cleveland Avenue terminal. Cars often attain 55 miles per hour on these sections and there are automatic train stops to halt trains passing red signals. There also are signals at the downtown terminal and to protect the lift section of the Steel Bridge. A number of switches in territory with signals are equipped with switch machines and are interlocked with the signals.

The signals are set for 2½ minute intervals between trains.

There are no block signals along the 2.2-mile downtown section or the 5.2-mile line on East Burnside Street. However, the traffic signals can be actuated by approaching cars at some downtown intersections and along the Burnside section, where the speed limit is 35 mph.

The yard at Ruby Junction has six maintenance tracks and five storage tracks. Direct suspension trolley wire was used on the downtown section but catenary was installed elsewhere.

A major effort was made to integrate the light rail line into the architectural tone of downtown Portland. Decorative pavement blocks were laid around the tracks and a distinctive design used for brick waiting shelters at stations outside the downtown area. The line passes through two historic districts on the west side of the Willamette River. At the three-track downtown terminal and storage yard on Southwest 11th Street, massive sculptured columns were used to distract the eye from the overhead trolley wire.

A plan to use rebuilt vintage streetcars through the downtown and over the Steel Bridge to Lloyd Center has been altered to use, instead, new cars built to look like historic Portland Traction Co. streetcars.

The downtown hub of the light rail system is Pioneer Square, a delightful plaza in the center of a downtown that has retained many pre-World War II buildings of distinguished architecture and texture. One of the great engineering monuments on the line is the massive Steel Bridge over the Willamette River. Besides the light rail line, it carries railroad tracks and has motor vehicle lanes.

The pioneering Portland-Oregon City line opened in 1893 is considered by many scholars to be the first electric interurban line in the United States. Two of that line's cars are shown on this page, a big wooden car reportedly built in the company shops in 1910, and assigned to a different Gresham line than today's route, and a lightweight steel car, below, built by Cincinnati Car Co. in 1925 for the Albany Southern Railway in New York and used by the Fonda, Johnstown & Gloversville before coming to Portland, where it served until the line was abandoned in 1958. On the page opposite is a narrow-gauged local Portland streetcar on the old Interstate Bridge over the Columbia River in 1937, and a 1,500-volt Southern Pacific suburban electric train in the 1920s.

RALPH W. DEMORO

A. J. BAKER

The light rail line enters downtown Portland on Southwest Morrison Street, with the principal city center stop being, above, at Broadway next to Pioneer Square, where the Pioneer Federal Court House with its dainty cupola serves as a backdrop. Until 1951, the historic Portland Hotel built by railroad magnate Henry Villard occupied the site of the square. The building above the train is the Meier & Frank Co. department store. The trains travel over an exclusive lane free of auto traffic on S.W. Morrison with the streetcar rails lined with paving blocks rescued when old streets were upgraded. A city ordinance requires that the blocks be salvaged and reused where appropriate for decorative purposes. The photo at left looks east on S.W. Morrison with Southwest Ninth Street in the foreground. On the page opposite, a downtown-bound train on Southwest First Avenue passes the New Market, one of the elegantly restored buildings served by the rail line as it passes through the Yamhill Historic District and the Skidmore/Old Town Historic District. Although Portland's weather is often soggy and occasionally frigid, many of the ticket machines are outside. The plaque is at the Pioneer Square station.

120
Portland

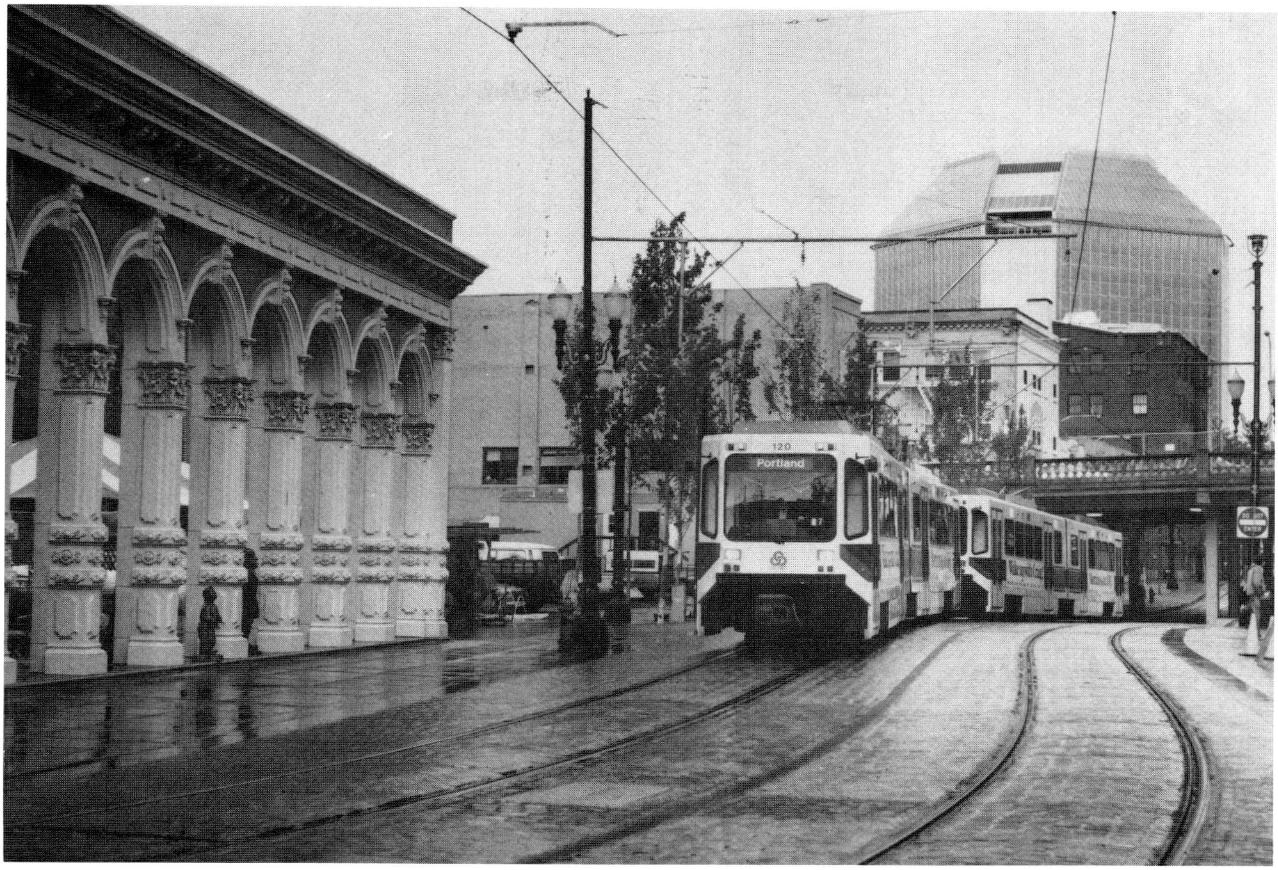

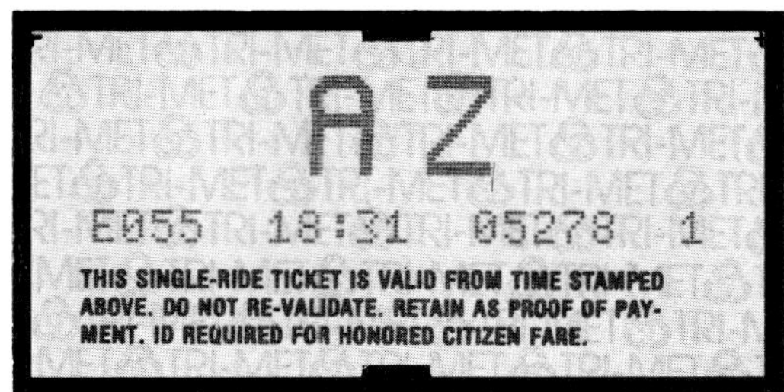

A Z
E055 18:31 05278 1
THIS SINGLE-RIDE TICKET IS VALID FROM TIME STAMPED ABOVE. DO NOT RE-VALIDATE. RETAIN AS PROOF OF PAYMENT. ID REQUIRED FOR HONORED CITIZEN FARE.

Tickets
TRI-MET
PURCHASE TICKET BEFORE BOARDING MAX
MAX AND BUS FARES ARE THE SAME
MAP
CASH FARES
SS SAVER FARES
PROOF OF PAYMENT
NOTE FARE DUE
INSERT COINS
INSERT BILLS
CANCEL
PRESS TICKET SELECTION BUTTON
$1,5,10 or 20
BILL RETURN
TAKE TICKET
CHANGE

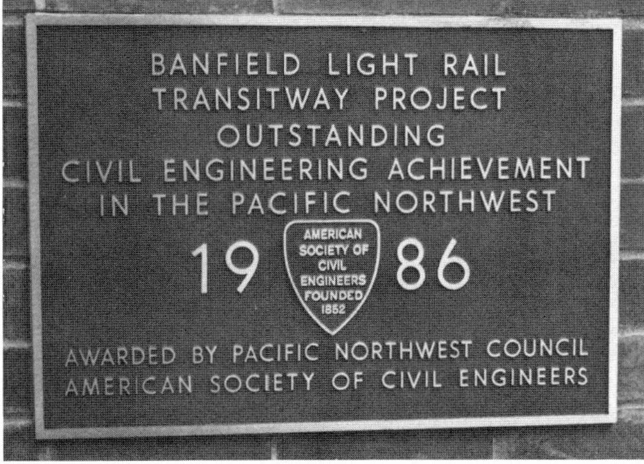

BANFIELD LIGHT RAIL
TRANSITWAY PROJECT
OUTSTANDING
CIVIL ENGINEERING ACHIEVEMENT
IN THE PACIFIC NORTHWEST
19 86
AMERICAN SOCIETY OF CIVIL ENGINEERS FOUNDED 1852
AWARDED BY PACIFIC NORTHWEST COUNCIL
AMERICAN SOCIETY OF CIVIL ENGINEERS

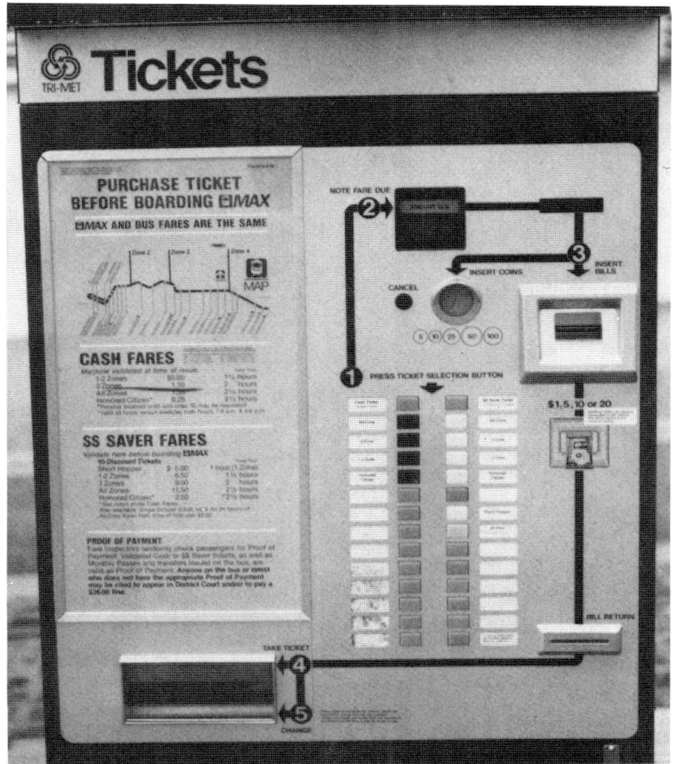

The Steel Bridge completed in 1912 by the Oregon-Washington Railway & Navigation Co., a subsidiary of the Union Pacific, carries the light rail line over the Willamette River and also accommodates Union Pacific, Burlington Northern, Amtrak and Southern Pacific trains, as well as motor vehicles. Its lower deck, carrying only railroad tracks, can be raised independently of the upper deck. On the page opposite, with the city skyline in the background, two trains pass on the eastern approach ramp. Below, a train on the downtown side of the bridge on free ride day, September 7, 1986, the day before revenue service began. In the first traction era, narrow-gauged streetcars ran in the same area as the light rail trains. Once over the bridge, on this page, the trains stop at Coliseum station below Interstate 5. The station, shown on the first day of revenue operation, serves the 13,000-seat Portland Memorial Coliseum, home of the Portland Trail Blazers basketball team. The Coliseum also has 100,000 square feet of exhibit space and the Ringling Brothers and Barnum & Bailey Circus calls there annually. Continuing east, below, the cars run on their own right of way the north curb lane of Northeast Holladay Street.

JOHN N. HARDER

HARRE W. DEMORO

The Lloyd Center station on Northeast Holladay Street at Holladay Park serves the big Lloyd Center shopping center, one of the largest in the United States. The center is built on a huge tract of land acquired early in the century by California oil tycoon Ralph B. Lloyd, who wanted to build a ''city within a city.'' Beyond Lloyd Center station, below, the cars roll over a short stretch of open track that takes them to the Banfield Freeway corridor. The two-car train is heading downtown on a rainy morning in April 1988.

After crossing the Union Pacific Railroad main line, the light rail tracks are situated between the railroad and the westbound lanes of the Banfield Freeway (Interstate 84) which cuts east-west through residential neighborhoods and an aging industrial section. The Hollywood station, above, serves a major retail zone surrounding the old Hollywood Theater, still a landmark on Northeast Sandy Boulevard. Note the wheelchair lift being used on the left. An eastbound train, below, accelerates from 60th Avenue station on November 8, 1986. The UP line is on the left.

After crossing Interstates 84 and 205, the light rail line swings south and stops at Gateway Station, above, on track that parallels Interstate 205. The station is named for a nearby shopping area and is used by a number of Tri-Met bus lines at left that connect with the trains. The station has three tracks, allowing extra service into the downtown. The viaduct crossing the two freeways is the largest all new structure on the rail system. Between Interstate 205 and Ruby Junction station, the line uses the median of East Burnside Street with the car controlling traffic signals at cross streets. The brick station, below, at Southeast 102nd Avenue, is typical of the passenger shelters along Burnside.

BOTH/HARRE W. DEMORO

HARRE W. DEMORO

East of Ruby Junction, the line is single track to Gresham City Hall, above, where it enters a passing siding for a short distance. On a rainy March 1988 afternoon, a downtown Portland-bound car approaches the station, which has a standard Portland MAX sign on the left. This is a 55-mile-per-hour section and was built on an old Portland Traction interurban right of way that had diesel-operated freight service into the 1980s. Below, the light rail line ends at the Gresham/Cleveland Avenue station, 15.1 miles from the 11th Avenue terminal in downtown Portland.

JOHN N. HARDER

Most of Portland's light rail car motormen are veteran Tri-Met bus drivers, like Bill Hunt, left, in the cab of downtown-bound car 104 in 1988. The controls are conveniently arranged on a console, and Hunt's left hand is on the handle that feeds power to the car's two electric motors, and also actuates the three braking systems. The round button above his right hand is for the emergency brake. Other buttons and switches are for doors, lights, heating and the automatic train control equipment that will stop a car if it passes a red signal. On the page opposite is the spacious rail car repair shop at Ruby Junction, big enough to handle 100 cars. The present 26-car fleet is stored outside in the weather in a 13-acre yard.

Portland's 26 articulated light rail cars, numbered 101-126, were designed by Constructiones Ferroviaries et Mettaliques, or BN, and built under license by Canadian-owned Bombardier Inc. at that firm's plant at Barre, Vt. The car is based on a pre-metro rail car built partly by BN for Rio de Janeiro. The La Bruqeoise et Nivelles trucks were built by BN and electrical equipment was supplied by a North American subisdiary of Swiss-based Brown Boveri Co. (BBC). Each car has two BBC model 4EL02060C traction motors. The control system is of the switched resistor type. The cars will accelerate and decelerate at 3 mph/sec. under normal conditions. They have dynamic, magnetic track and disk brakes that are spring applied and hydraulic released. There is a small air compressor to operate the sander; the rest of the car is electric. The car is 86' 11¾'' long over anticlimbers, 89.14' long over coupler faces, 8'8'' wide, weighs 92,150 pounds, seats 76, is designed for 750-volt operation (range 525 to 875 volts), and has a top speed of 55 mph. The car is not air conditioned. The coupler is a Dellner Type 35. The car contract was awarded in September 1981 and the first underframe was started at Barre in the fall of 1982, with the first car shell assembled in December 1982. Car 101 moved under its own power at the plant in November 1983, and the 101 and 103 were tested at the U.S. Department of Transportation Test Track at Pueblo, Colo., from December 1983 through March 1984. Car 103 was the first car delivered to Portland, arriving in April 1984. The last car was accepted in October 1986. Portland's track gauge is 4' 8½.''

Portland's BN-style cars have spacious and bright interiors with padded seats. Although there are seats for 76 passengers, under a crush load condition, each car can carry 211 passengers. The protruding coupler and high floor shown in the view below are evidence that the car is a descendant of the Rio pre-metro car, which shares track with large rapid transit trains. Note how the plug doors fit tightly into the carbody when they are closed.

After departing the Watt/80 terminal of the north line, Sacramento's RT Metro trains run on private right of way between Interstate 80, on the right, and lanes of a never opened freeway on the left, now used for rail station parking lots. There is enough room on the right for a second track. Below, on the K Street mall downtown, a train bound for Watt/80 approaches the Cathedral Square station at 11th Street. The station takes its name from the Cathedral of the Blessed Sacrament, far right, the mother church of the Catholic Diocese of Sacramento. In an attempt to revive the downtown area, K Street was closed to vehicular traffic in 1965 and converted into a pedestrian mall, but the effort did not reverse the trend.

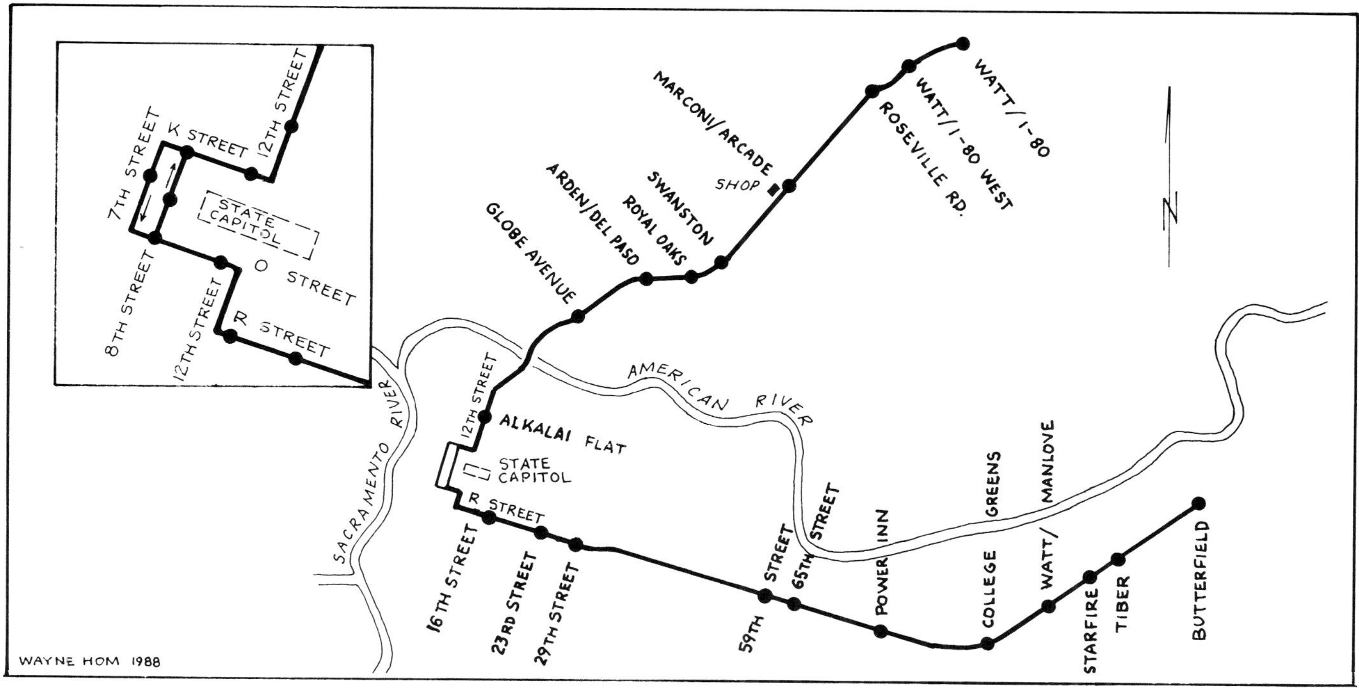

Sacramento

RT Metro, Sacramento's light rail system, is operated by the Sacramento Regional Transit District, which also runs the 212-vehicle local bus system. The combined rail and bus system carries about 55,000 passengers a day, with more than 13,000 of the total being on the rail line, which was built to carry 20,500 riders a day.

The system opened in two stages. The nine-mile section from Watt/80 through the downtown to 12th Street station near R Street opened on March 12, 1987, and is usually referred to as the North line. The 9.3-mile Folsom line, or East line, was opened on September 5, 1987.

About two-thirds of the 18.3-mile system is single track. This limits the line to a maximum of eight trains running at a frequency of 15 minutes. A considerable level of coordination is required to assure that trains pass on double-tracked sections. A further limiting factor is that 2.5 miles of the system are in city streets. Except in the downtown, the lines are protected by automatic block signals. There are no provisions to stop trains passing red signals.

Direct suspension wire is used for city street operation and catenary was installed elsewhere. The system uses 750 volts DC supplied from 14 substations.

In a major effort to minimize disruption, existing rights of way were used where possible. Most of the line between Watt/80 and Roseville Road uses an alignment for a freeway that was not comp-leted. The station parking lots were built on the unused freeway lanes. South of Roseville Road, bridges and right of way intended for a freeway were used. Between Royal Oaks and Del Paso stations, the line is on an abandoned Sacramento Northern Railway branch. The SN had abandoned the line, which had been retained for freight service after passenger operations were discontinued in 1933, but the track was still intact. A portion of an existing highway bridge north of the downtown was used to cross the American River and the Union Pacific (former Western Pacific) tracks.

The Folsom line follows the alignment of the Southern Pacific's Placerville branch, which was abandoned between the downtown and about 65th Street. East of 65th Street, the light rail line parallels the SP line, which was relocated at some locations.

Through the downtown retail section, the line runs on the K Street Mall which has been closed to vehicular traffic. On sections of 12th Street and on Seventh and Eighth and O streets, the tracks are laid on the side of the street next to the curb.

Two major bridges, both built as single-tracked structures, were erected on the Folsom line. The Bee Bridge, named for the nearby office and plant of the city's major newspaper, the *Sacramento Bee*, carries the line over a number of streets and the Union Pacific (old Western Pacific) main line. The second bridge, much more spectacular, takes the eastbound trains under U.S. 50, over the SP Stockton main line and Placerville branch, and under high voltage power lines.

The abandonment of the in-city section of the SP branch resulted in an unusual arrangement to continue rail freight service to the *Bee*. RT Metro contracted with Union Pacific to switch cars of newsprint to the newspaper plant on a new spur from the nearby UP line.

California's capital city has a long and rich history of electric traction and was at the center of the Sacramento Northern Railway's 353-mile interurban network that stretched from San Francisco to Chico in the northern Sacramento Valley. A Sacramento-Woodland local train, below, approached the Tower Bridge over the Sacramento River in 1939. In the view above, taken in 1940 only a city block from the present light rail line on 12th Street, a San Francisco-bound train awaits departure time at Union Station at 11th and I Streets, which became a supermarket and bus station after SN abandoned interurban operations in the Sacramento area in October 1940.

L. L. BONNEY

Sacramento's three streetcar systems were merged into Sacramento City Lines during World War II. The new company, owned by pro-bus Pacific City Lines, operated the lines formerly owned by the Pacific Gas & Electric Co., Sacramento Northern and Central California Traction Co. until 1947. A former CCT car, built originally for Fresno Traction, was on a railfan excursion, above, in 1946. Note how the doors had been closed when conductors were removed in Fresno and the car converted to one-man operation. A PG&E car with open sections for the hot valley summers is shown below in 1938 when the electric utility still owned the system.

RALPH W. DEMORO

JOHN N. HARDER

A drizzle that turned to a downpour didn't dampen RT Metro's opening day ceremonies on March 12, 1987. The first train broke through a big banner, above, at the Watt/80 station then headed downtown. There was an elaborate ceremony, below, at Del Paso station, with Congressman Vic Fazio, a light rail supporter, and Adriana Gianturco, former director of the California Department of Transportation, among those at the podium. The track is laid on the old Swanston Branch of the Sacramento Northern Railway, which had electric passenger service from 1914 to 1933. The line, retained for freight service, had been abandoned when RT Metro took over the right of way but the tracks were still there.

HARRE W. DEMORO

HARRE W. DEMORO

The Swanston station was built next to the Southern Pacific's Overland Route main line, right, and is named for the family that ran a meatpacking company in the area from 1914 into the 1940's. The plant was surrounded by a 2,800-acre cattle ranch. The two-car train has just left a double-track section and is arriving at Swanston Station. In the background is the El Camino Avenue overpass. The landscaping and parking lot on the left are typical RT Metro features. At Arden Way and Del Paso Boulevard, below, the trains leave the former Sacramento Northern Railway interurban right of way and turn onto Del Paso Avenue, where they run in a paved area in the center of the street. The Del Paso station is behind the train. This area was once a separate community called North Sacramento but is now part of the city of Sacramento.

JOHN N. HARDER

RT Metro Map
PACIFIC GRACE

MACHINE DOES NOT GIVE CHANGE
INSERT COINS
$ 1.00 / .50 / .25 / .10 / .05
COIN CANCEL
OVERPAY
SELECT FARE
BEFORE PAYING
RT METRO
TICKETS
BOLETOS
1 SELECT FARE
PEAK: 6-9 A.M. & 3:30-6 P.M. WEEKDAYS
OFF PEAK: ALL OTHER TIMES
Seleccione el pasaje
HORARIO - PICO
6-9 A.M. & 3:30-6 P.M. DIAS DE SEMANA
HORARIO NORMAL: TODAS LAS DEMAS HORAS
2 DEPOSIT EXACT CHANGE
MACHINE DOES NOT GIVE CHANGE
Deposite el pasaje exacto
ESTA MAQUINA NO DA CAMBIO
3 TAKE TICKET BELOW
RETAIN THROUGHOUT ENTIRE RIDE
Tome el boleto abajo
CONSERVE DURANTE TODO EL RECORRIDO
PEAK FARE
OFF-PEAK FARE
ADULT
STUDENT
SENIOR CITIZEN
DISABLED
ADULT
STUDENT
SENIOR CITIZEN
DISABLED
CBD
MORE THAN ONE TICKET
VALIDACIÓN DE BOLETOS
PAGADOS DE ANTEMANO: ABAJO
PREPAID TICKET
VALIDATION BELOW
xarmax
CH - 8050 Zürich
TAKE TICKET
TICKET BOOKS ONLY

BOTH/JOHN N. HARDER

Because RT Metro uses the honor system and has no fareboxes on the cars, fare inspectors, like ex-bus driver Joe Velasquez, page opposite, are assigned to roam the cars and ask passengers to show their tickets. Passengers without tickets pay a fine of up to $250 and there are few offenders. San Diego, Portland and San Jose have the same system. The ticket machines, below, have instructions in English and Spanish and don't make change. After leaving the Globe station, above, the trains veer onto curving private right of way that takes them to the Highway 160 bridge that carries the rail line and motor vehicle traffic over the American River and the Union Pacific main line. In downtown Sacramento, along the K Street mall which is used only by the rail line and pedestrians, RT Metro trains pass the elegant old Weinstock's Department Store building with its arched grand entryway. The building has been remodeled for offices. Planners hope that the light rail line will bring new life to the street.

Northbound cars operating on Eighth Street pass within two blocks of California's Roman-Corinthian-style Capitol, built between 1860 and 1874, when most of the Golden State was a howling wilderness. The Capitol is at the end of Capitol Mall, formerly M Street. The pole alongside the train is milepost zero, with the Watt/80 line on the left and the Butterfield, or Folsom line on the right. Until 1940, Sacramento Northern interurban trains from San Francisco and the Woodland branch turned from M Street onto Eighth Street, which also was served by Central California Traction Co. interurbans from Stockton until 1933 and CCT streetcars into the 1940s. Because of the 100-degree dry summer weather, trees were planted in pre-air conditioner days along downtown streets and much of the older sections of Sacramento are still tree-shaded, as depicted below at Eighth and N streets. Track laid next to the curb is a characteristic of much of the city street sections of the Sacramento light rail system.

BOTH/JOHN N. HARDER

The Folsom line follows the alignment of California's first common carrier railroad, the Sacramento Valley Railroad, which became Southern Pacific's Placerville branch. With the coming of the light rail line, SP abandoned the branch west of approximately the 65th Street RT Metro station, and the transit system relocated some sections of the freight-only line that remained and at other locations laid track alongside the existing railroad. Near the center of the city, above, the line runs through an old industrial and residential area. A downtown-bound car has just crossed 17th Street and is approaching the 16th Street station. The Folsom line's Watt/Manlove station, below, serves the Rosemont residential neighborhood. This is a typical RT Metro stop, with a short canopy covered with a sheet metal roof, benches and, at the left, a ticket machine and change maker. Passengers are offered only little protection from the elements at Sacramento RT Metro stations because summers are hot and winters occasionally icy. A slight dusting of snow is a rare event.

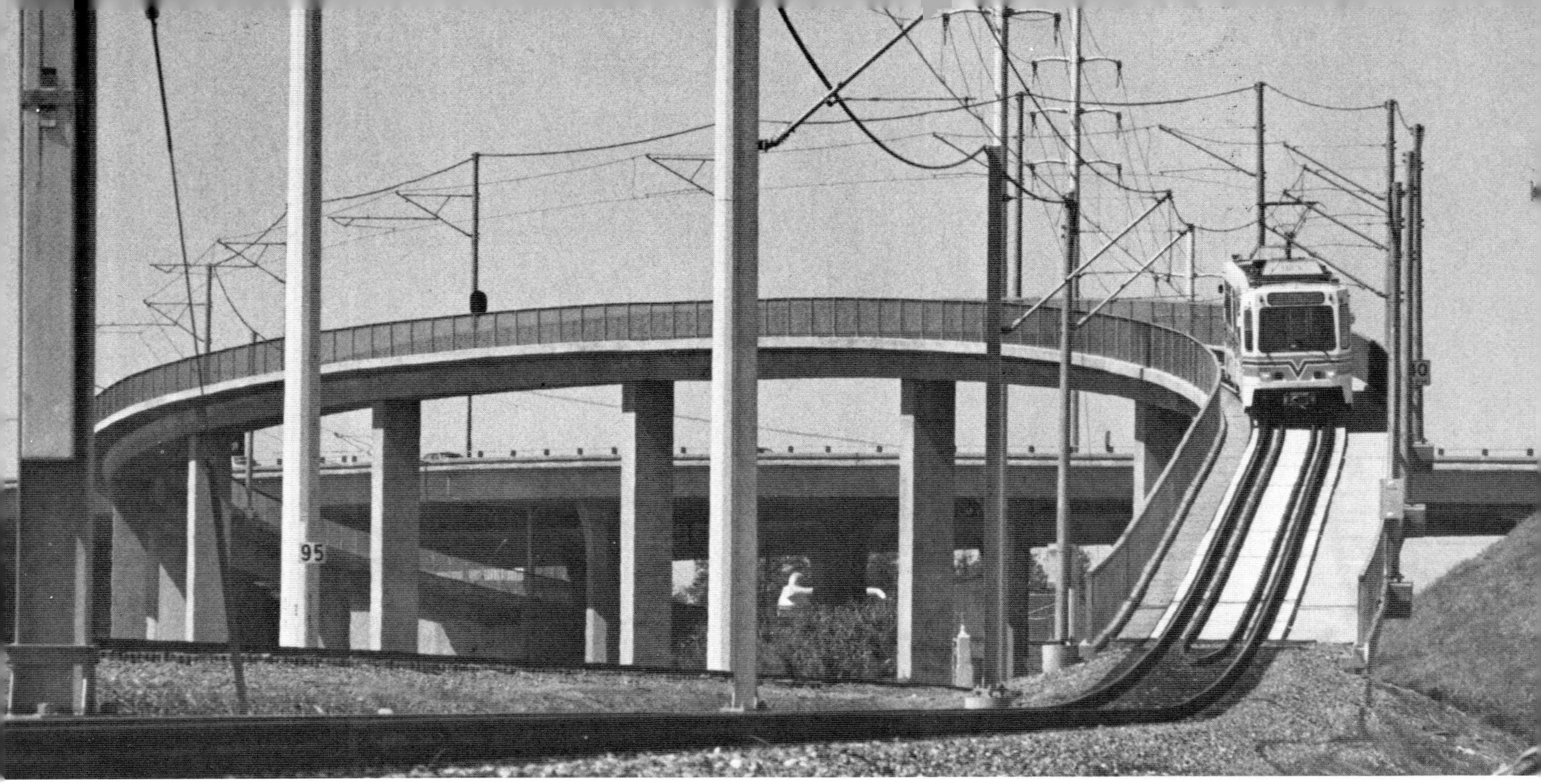

DONALD R. KAPLAN

JOHN N. HARDER

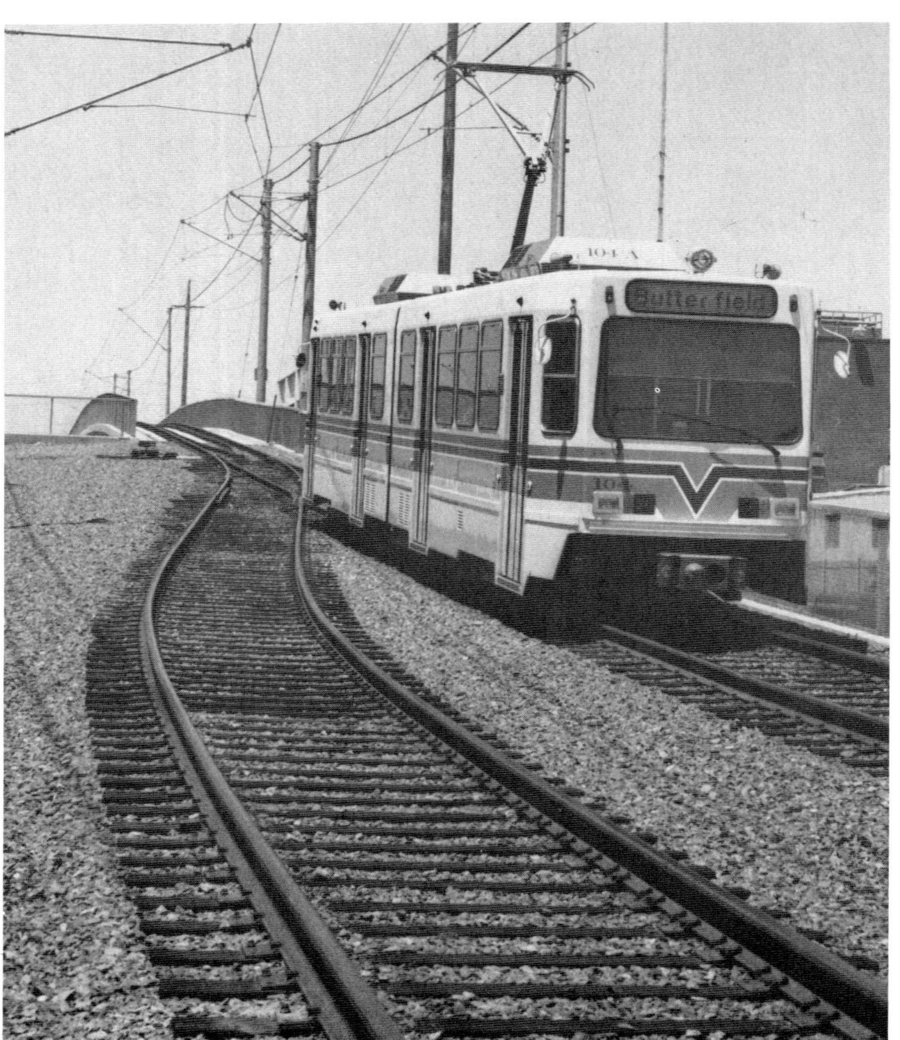

Spectacular bridges are a feature of the Folsom line, with the roller-coaster Brighton Bridge, above, standing out as a major engineering and esthetic landmark. The Butterfield-bound train is about to leave the bridge which carries the tracks under Highway 50, over the Southern Pacific main line to Stockton and the SP Placerville branch, and finally under an 115,000-volt power line owned by the Sacramento Municipal Utility District. Another Folsom line structure, on the left, is called the Bee Bridge, named for the *Sacramento Bee,* the City's major daily newspaper, which has its editorial offices and printing plant next to the tracks. This bridge carries RT Metro trains over 19th, 20, 21st and 22nd streets and the Union Pacific main line. The downtown-bound car has just left the 23rd Street station.

JOHN N. HARDER

Near the Power Inn station on the Folsom line, there still are patches of open country and the single-tracked light rail line paralleling the SP's Placerville branch takes on the look of an old electric interurban railway that has escaped the automobile age. The silos at Jackson Road behind the car and the open field on the right are relics of a slower age. RT Metro's bright new shop, below, is adjacent to the Marconi station. The picture was taken in 1986 before the system opened and while the first few Siemens-Duewag cars were being checked over by factory technicians. This explains the presence of the pickup truck.

HARRE W. DEMORO

Siemens-Duewag restyled the U2 body for the 26 U2A type cars it delivered to Sacramento in 1986. Except for the different end and the fixed low steps, the air conditioned cars are near duplicates of the Edmonton, Calgary and San Diego cars. The 750-volt Sacramento cars seat 64 passengers and are 79' 6'' long over couplers and 8' 10'' wide. They weigh 78,000 pounds and have Siemens cam control and two Siemens type 1KB2021 traction motors. The cars have dynamic and magnetic track brakes and spring-applied, electrically released disk friction brakes. Sacramento's cars will accelerate and decelerate at 3 mph/sec. and have a top speed of 50 miles per hour. All but one of the cars were assembled in Sacramento; car 101 arrived complete from Germany. The roof-mounted air conditioning is evident on car 120, above, shown in March 1987, the month the system opened. The front view, left, was taken of the 102 in June 1986 when acceptance testing was beginning on a short section of track near the shops and yard and shows the Dellner coupler. There are subtle differences in the interiors of the Sacramento U2 car, page opposite, and San Diego's first cars, shown on page 45. Fittings on the stanchions are different and the ceiling shape flatter to accommodate ducts for Sacramento's air conditioning. Sacramento's cab doors have windows and the articulation is more rounded on the San Diego car. The console is typical of U2 cars, with the power and brake handle on the far left. The motorman must depress a button on the floor to operate the car. This is a safety measure called "deadman control" and will stop the car if the operator is disabled and removes his foot from the device. Sacramento's track gauge is 4' 8½''.

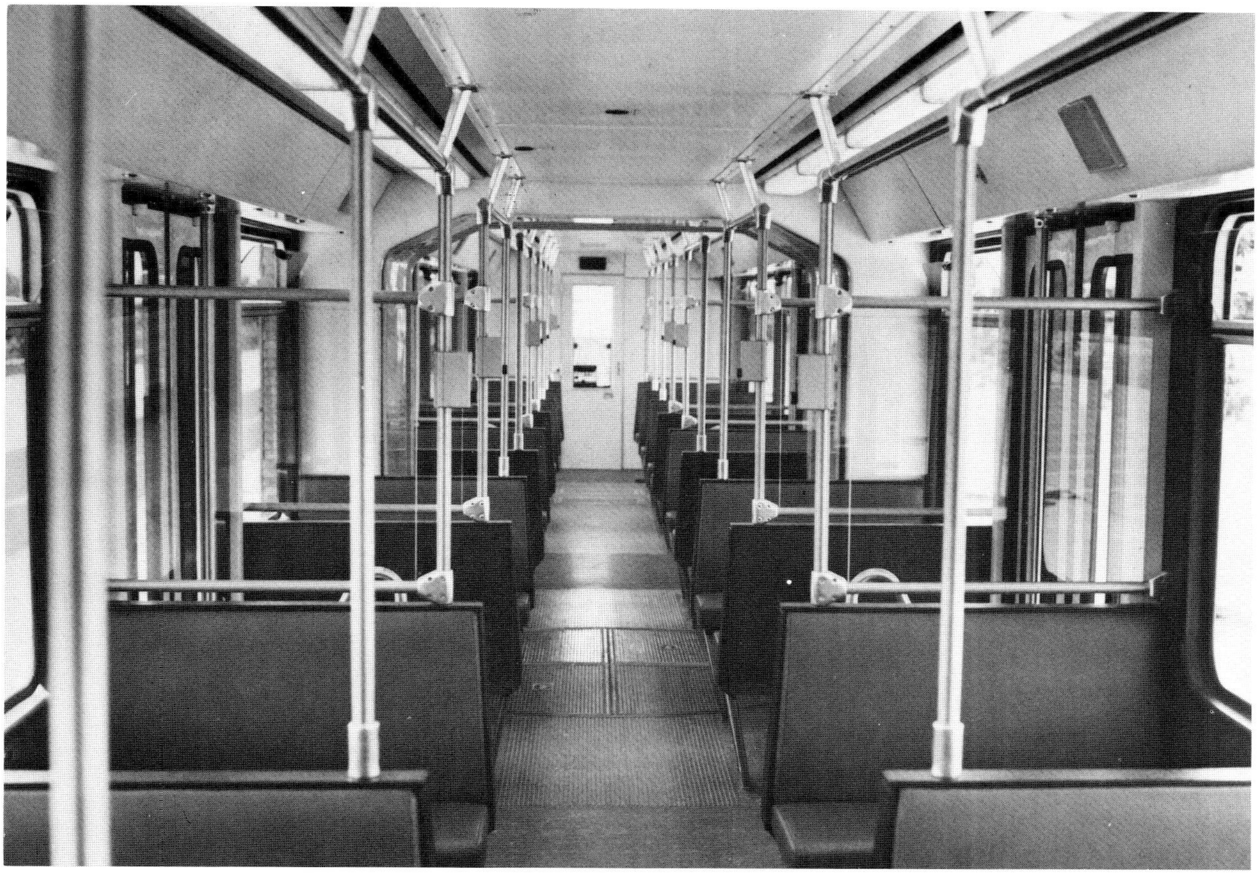

HARRE W. DEMORO

DONALD R. KAPLAN

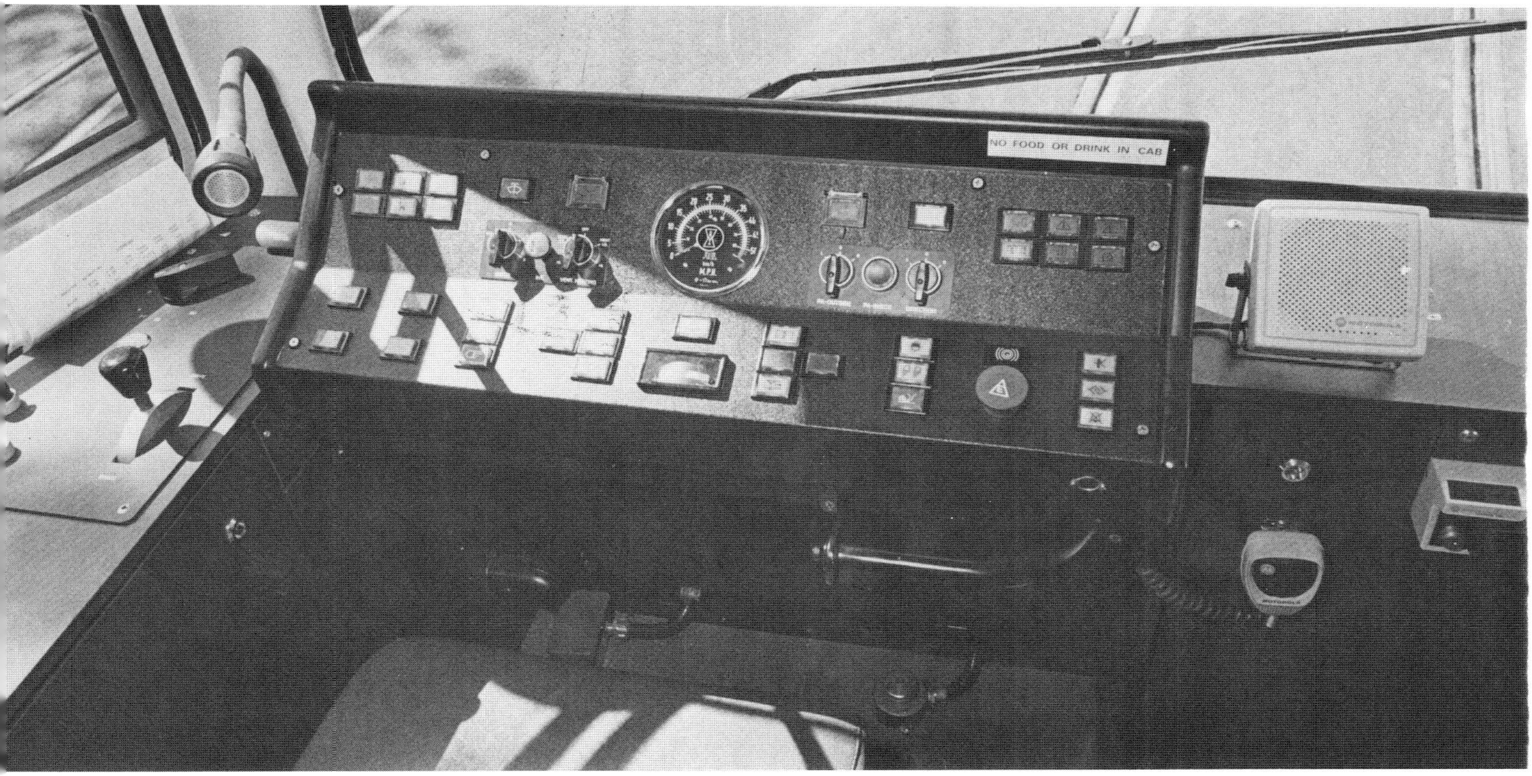

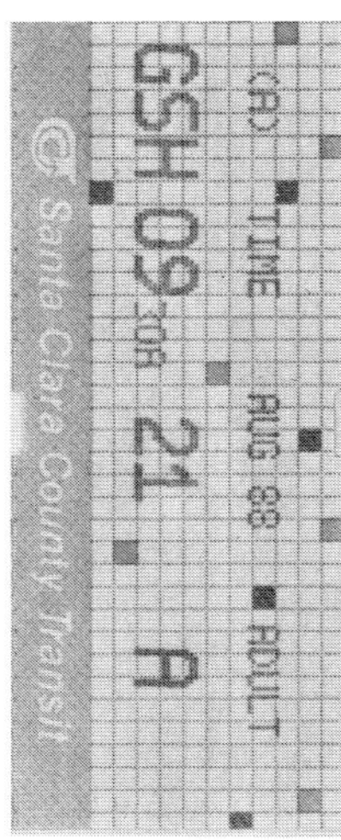

From December 11, 1987, until the downtown section was opened on June 17, 1988, the San Jose light rail line terminated, above, on Younger Street on tracks leading to the system's shop and storage yard. One of the project's major supporters, Santa Clara County Supervisor Rod Diridon, in coat and tie, is exiting one of the gleaming new cars on December 19, 1987. Near Great America station on the north end of the line, left, the tracks cross San Tomas Aquino Creek as they follow Tasman Drive to the city of Santa Clara's convention center. Great America station serves an amusement park of the same name.

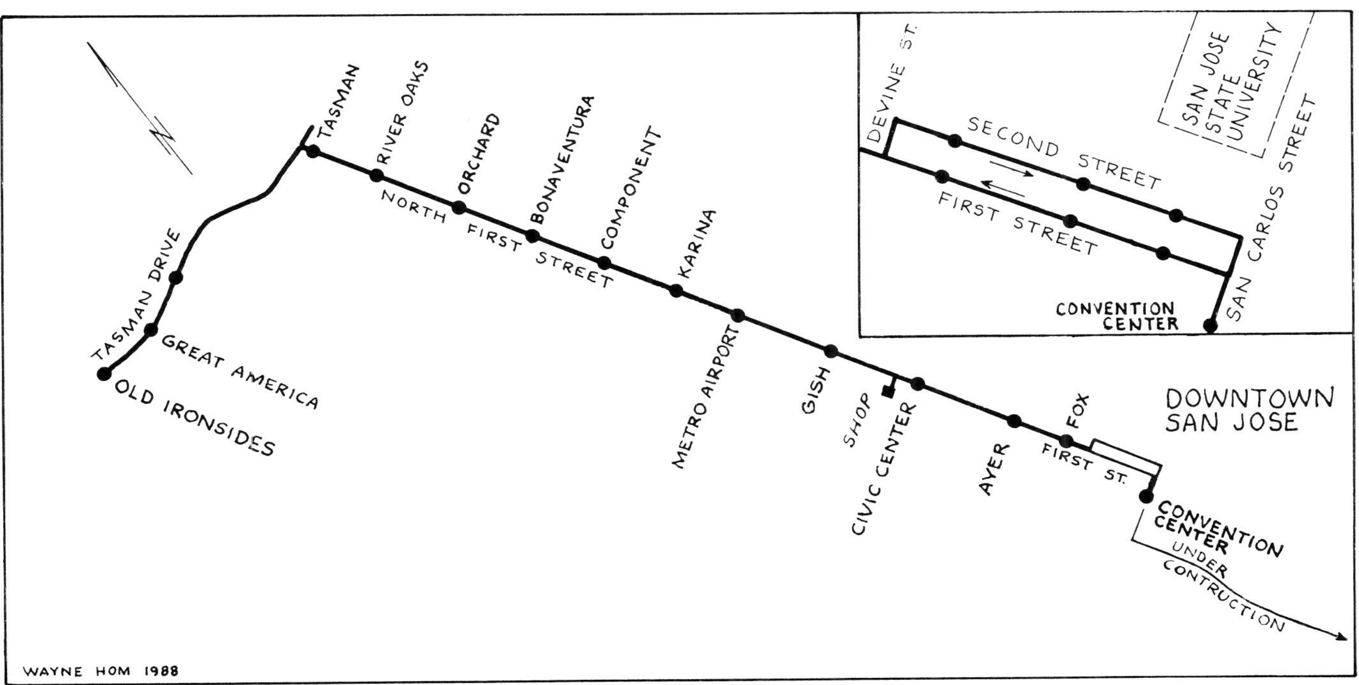

San Jose

The Santa Clara County Transportation Agency is building the 20-mile Guadalupe Light Rail Project, which derives its name from a river that roughly parallels much of the route. The county agency also operates a regional bus system that carries about 120,000 riders per day with about 540 vehicles.

The line is opening in phases and the nine-mile section now in operation does not serve the areas south of San Jose which are expected to generate most of the expected 20,000 daily riders. A 6.5-mile section between Old Ironsides and a temporary station near the shops at Younger Street opened on December 11, 1987, but carried fewer than 1,000 riders a day. The section into the downtown which runs between Younger Street and Convention Center station opened on June 17, 1988.

While construction continues on the remaining section south from San Jose, the completion date is uncertain because of a lawsuit dealing with an adjacent highway project. Both RT Metro in Sacramento and the MAX system in Portland have considered leasing some of San Jose's cars until the full Santa Clara line is operating.

When completed, probably in the early 1990's, the line will run to Santa Teresa south of the city and near a large IBM plant. There also will be a short branch over an old Southern Pacific route to Almaden. The completed system will have 33 stations and is designed for 21 trains totaling 44 cars to operate simultaneously.

The San Jose system is double tracked. The section operating in 1988 did not have block signals (except for terminal signals at Old Ironsides) but the high-speed (55 miles per hour) sections south of San Jose will have signals, but not automatic stops. The overhead trolley voltage is 750 DC. Direct suspension wire is used downtown and catenary elsewhere.

A major feature of the newly opened section is the 14-block transit mall in downtown San Jose, which the rail cars loop through. The mall is part of a $1 billion redevelopment effort to revive the downtown, which declined after World War II. A non-profit corporation, San Jose Trolley Corp., is restoring six vintage streetcars and will operate them through the downtown on the same tracks used by the light rail cars.

The northern part of the line runs through the San Jose Golden Triangle section of high technology manufacturing, an area in transition, with the cars passing new industrial plants and alfalfa fields. At Great America station in the city of Santa Clara, the line serves both the Great America amusement park and the city of Santa Clara Convention Center. As the line approaches downtown San Jose from the north, it dips under the Southern Pacific's freight-only San Jose-Milpitas-Oakland line in an underpass. Most of the light rail line south of downtown San Jose will run in the center of a new nine-mile freeway.

The delays and questionable estimates of ultimate ridership have resulted in less than positive publicity for the system. One of the most embarrassing incidents involved the effort to name car 804 by conducting a contest. The winning entry was "Challenger," but officials secretly changed the name to "Challenge" because of the recent Space Shuttle disaster. Soon, the secret was in the newspaper, much to the displeasure of the light rail management.

SAN JOSE - LOS GATOS INTERURBAN RY. CO.
16

Streetcar and interurban systems owned by Southern Pacific served San Jose and the surrounding area, and the city had streetcars until 1938. A car destined for the city of Santa Clara, above, was about to switch from East Santa Clara Street to North First Street during the final days of rail operation. One of San Jose's 32 two-axle Birney Safety Cars, is shown below in the early 1930s. On the page opposite, top, is a Peninsular Railway interurban car built originally for the San Jose-Los Gatos Interurban Railway and, below, one of that line's local cars. The Peninsular was abandoned in 1934, but the big car has been restored at the Western Railway Museum at Rio Vista Junction north of San Francisco.

Until rails can be pushed south from downtown San Jose, the line will end at the Convention Center station which serves, above, the 1934 vintage San Jose Civic Auditorium on West San Carlos Street at South Market Street. On South Second Street, below, the trains run next to the sidewalk in a new transit mall. The Convention Center-bound train is about to swing into East San Carlos Street. The Civic Auditorium's Spanish Colonial Revival architecture recalls San Jose's Spanish and Mexican roots, when the area was part of Alta California.

The light rail line is part of a major effort by San Jose officials to revive the city's downtown and the cars loop through an area of empty old stores and glistening office towers and pass a new Fairmont Hotel. On North Second Street at Santa Clara Street, above, a two-car train heading for the Convention Center station rolls over the new transit mall that puts the light rail cars up against the sidewalk. North of downtown, on North First Street at Julian Street, a southbound car has exited the underpass beneath Southern Pacific's freight-only Milpitas line.

BOTH PAGES/JOHN N. HARDER

The Santa Clara County light rail line links the San Jose of the 18th and 19th centuries with the city's high technology present. Founded in 1777 by the Spanish, San Jose is California's oldest town, as distinguished from military installations and missions, and was the first state capital. In the view above, a northbound test car stops on North First Street at the St. James Park station, which serves both the park, an early hub of the city, and the old Santa Clara County Court House, built in 1866. The modern San Jose of a much faster era is depicted below with a southbound car darting along the North First Street median at appropriately named Component Drive station in the city's high tech Silicon Valley manufacturing district. The wire fence on the left was installed as a temporary safety measure during high-speed testing of the new cars. Another example of modern San Jose is on the page opposite: Three languages on ticket machines and schedules, English, Spanish, and Vietnamese. The line's spacious new shop is shown below. All 50 cars can be stored and maintained on the 18-acre site, and the facility can be expanded to handle 100 cars.

JOHN N. HARDER

HARRE W. DEMORO

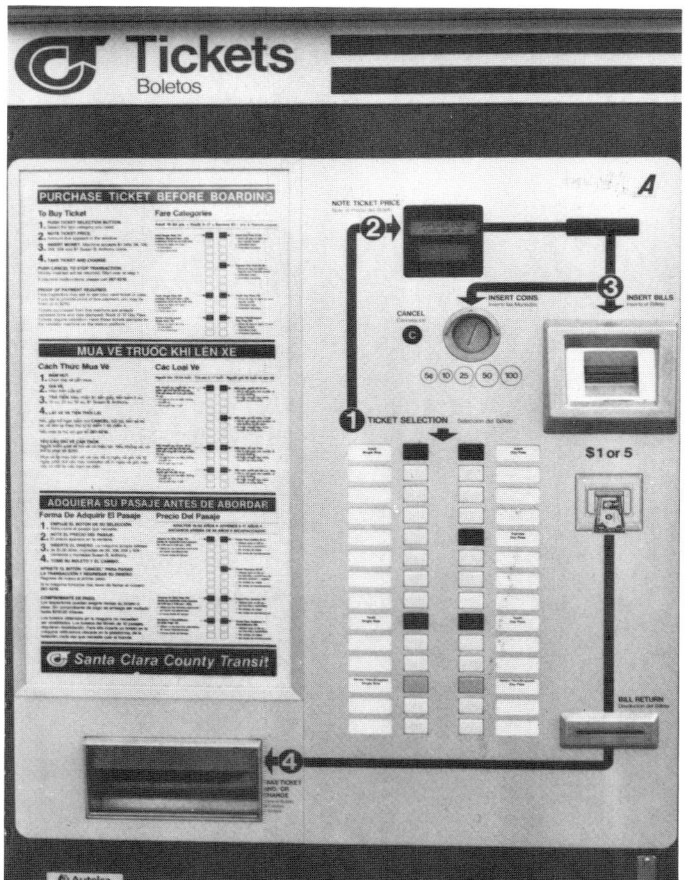

LIGHT RAIL INFORMATION

PURCHASE TICKET BEFORE BOARDING

WELCOME TO YOUR LIGHT RAIL TRANSIT SYSTEM. All riders must have a valid ticket or pass before boarding. You can purchase Books of 10 Day Pass Tickets and Monthly Flash Passes at sales outlets. Or buy a Single Ride Ticket or Day Pass from the station vending machine.

BOARD THE VEHICLE. Always stand behind the grooved, yellow tile safety band until the light rail vehicle comes to a complete stop. Push the green button beside the doorway to enter.

WHILE ON THE VEHICLE. Always remain seated or hold handrails while vehicle is in motion. Don't stand or sit on the steps. Please move to the door as the train comes to your stop.

EXIT THE VEHICLE. Locate your stop on the system map inside each vehicle. When the vehicle stops, push the green button on the pole nearest the doors to exit.

PROOF OF PAYMENT REQUIRED. On-board fare inspectors may ask to see your valid ticket or pass. Failure to have proof of payment or show it to the fare inspector could result in a fine of up to $250 (Penal Code Section 640).

SPECIAL ACCESS FOR SPECIAL NEEDS.
- In June 1988, light rail stations will have mechanical lifts to assist wheelchair users and others with limited mobility. Two wheelchair tiedowns per vehicle will be provided.
- Conveniently located seats are designated for elderly and disabled riders.
- The yellow tile safety band running along the station platform is grooved for identification by visually impaired persons.
- Ticket vending machine information will be available in Braille in March 1988.

SAFETY FIRST. Remembering a few important rules will make your trip safe and convenient.
- Stop, look and listen. Light rail vehicles move quickly and quietly.
- Never walk in the trackway, except within crosswalks.
- Cross only at signalized intersections.
- Let the light rail vehicle leave the station before you enter the crosswalk.
- Always watch out for cars.
- Be careful in construction areas.
- Wait behind the grooved, yellow tile safety band until the light rail vehicle has come to a complete stop.
- Stay seated or hold handrails while vehicle is in motion.
- In emergency situations, use the intercom to contact the driver and follow his/her instructions.

TIME SCHEDULE

USING THIS TIME SCHEDULE. Column headings (locations) are called "timepoints." To determine departure times for your light rail stop, find the timepoint on the route map nearest to and before your stop and check the times below. All "p.m." times are shown in bold numbers.

TIN TỨC XE ĐIỆN

MUA VÉ TRƯỚC KHI LÊN XE

CHÀO MỪNG QUI VỊ. Hành khách cần có vé còn hiệu lực để lên xe. Quý vị có thể mua Vé dài hạn: Vé tháng hay Vé 10 Ngày tại những nơi bán vé (gọi số 287-4210 để biết địa điểm bán vé gần nhất). Hoặc vé ngắn hạn: Vé một ngày, hay vé 2 giờ, bán tại các Máy Bán Vé có đặt tại các trạm xe điện.

TRƯỚC KHI LÊN XE. Luôn luôn đứng sau hàng gạch màu vàng, vạch an toàn, chờ xe dừng hẳn lại. Bấm nút đèn xanh bên cạnh cửa, cửa mở, lên xe.

TRONG XE. Khi xe đang chạy, ngồi tại ghế, nếu phải đứng cần vịn cho chặt. Không đứng hay ngồi tại cầu thang lên xuống.

XUỐNG XE. Trong xe, có Bản đồ các trạm xe. Khi gần đến trạm cần xuống, xeo dây chuông để tài xế dừng lại. Khi xe dừng hẳn lại, bấm nút đèn xanh nơi cửa ra vào gần nhất, cửa mở, xuống xe cẩn thận.

GIỮ CẨN THẬN VÉ CÒN HIỆU LỰC. Phải có vé còn hiệu lực, để trình cho người soát vé, nếu không có, có thể bị phạt tới $250 (Luật phạt số 640).

NGƯỜI GIÀ YẾU, HOẶC NGƯỜI ĐI XE LĂN, LÊN XUỐNG XE ĐIỆN.
- Kể từ tháng 6, 1988, sẽ có trang bị máy móc giúp đỡ người già yếu, hoặc xe lăn, lên và xuống xe. Trong xe, có 2 chỗ đặc biệt dành cho người xe lăn.
- Chỗ ngồi tiện nghi cho người già, hoặc tàn tật.
- Hàng gạch màu vàng, vạch an toàn; người mắt rất kém biết được bằng chân của họ.
- Kể từ tháng 3, 1988, trên máy bán vé sẽ có phần chỉ dẫn cho người mắt rất kém. Họ đọc bằng những ngón tay.

LUẬT LỆ AN TOÀN. Nhớ áp dụng luật lệ này, để di chuyển an toàn mãi.
- Dừng lại, nhìn và lắng nghe. Xe nhanh và êm.
- Không bao giờ băng qua đường trừ đường dành cho người đi bộ.
- Chỉ băng qua nơi ngả ba, hoặc hệ thống đèn.
- Để xe chạy khỏi sân ga, sau đó vào đường dành cho người đi bộ.
- Luôn luôn nhìn kỹ xe Điện và xe.
- Cẩn thận trong những vùng còn cất.
- Tại sân ga, đứng chờ sau hàng vàng, chờ xe tới và dừng hẳn lại.
- Khi xe đang chạy, ngồi tại ghế, đứng, cần vịn cho chặt.
- Trường hợp khẩn cấp, dùng máy chuyện với tài xế, và tuân theo của họ.

The 50 Santa Clara County cars, numbered 801-850, were built by Canadian-owned UTDC in 1986-87, and are based on an articulated car the company had developed for Toronto. The San Jose (Santa Clara County) carbody is 86' 8'' long and the car is 88' 6'' over coupler faces. The body is 8' 8½'' inches wide. Features include air suspension and air conditioning. The 750-volt cars will accelerate at 3.0 mph/sec. and decelerate at 3.5 mph/sec. They weigh about 100,000 pounds and have a top speed of 65 miles an hour, but are restricted to 55 mph. The cars have dynamic, disk and magnetic track brakes, with the disk brake being spring applied and air released. The BBC electric equipment includes switched resistor control and two model 4EL02060C traction motors. The motors were built in the United States under subcontract by Reliance Electric. Cars 802 and 803 were built at UTDC's Thunder Bay, Ontario, plant and shipped complete to San Jose after testing at Pueblo, Colorado. The rest were shipped disassembled from Thunder Bay without trucks and air conditioning to the former San Jose Steel Co. plant for final assembly. The trucks were assembled in Sacramento. The cars have Ohio Brass Form 85 couplers, M.A.N. SECTA type inboard bearing trucks and an articulated joint built by M.A.N. There are 75 seats. The track gauge is 4' 8½''.

Resistors for acceleration and braking and the air conditioning equipment are mounted on the roof, shielded from view by a shroud to improve the appearance of the San Jose car. Note the electronic destination sign and folding doors. The 75-seat car is designed for 166 passengers and can accommodate 257 during crush load conditions. Because of their weight and air suspension, these are probably the smoothest riding light rail cars in the West.

Ground was broken for the Los Angeles-Long Beach light rail line on October 31, 1985. Wielding shovels on that historic day were, from left, Jacki Bacharach, chairperson of the Los Angeles County Transportation Commission, LACTC Commissioner and County Supervisor Deane Dana, Los Angeles Mayor Tom Bradley, Los Angeles Councilmember Joan Milke Flores, and LACTC Commissioner and County Supervisor Kenneth Hahn. One of the first major projects to get under way was, below, the repair shop and yard. After light rail construction started, the LACTC modified its plan and now intends to build the Century Freeway line as an automated rail system rather than with light rail technology, so this shop may have two types of rolling stock in a number of years.

LACTC

ANN REEVES/LACTC

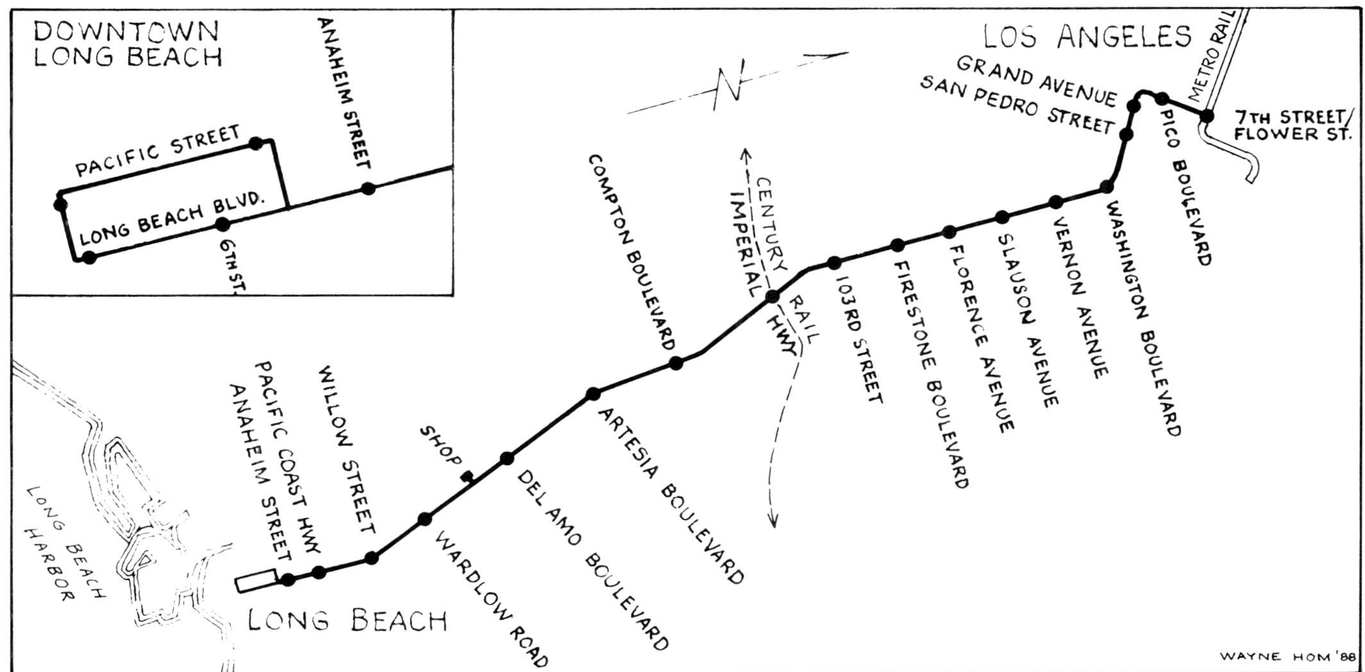

Los Angeles

The 21.5-mile Los Angeles-Long Beach line is being built by the Los Angeles County Transportation Commission, and is due to open, perhaps only in part, in July 1990. The LACTC is a county-wide planning, construction and finance agency, but not an operating district. It is expected that the rail line will be operated by the Southern California Rapid Transit District (RTD), which runs the major Los Angeles area bus system. RTD carries about 1.7 million riders a day on about 2,000 buses.

The Los Angeles-Long Beach line is one of the most ambitious new light rail projects in the Western United States. Only the Muni Metro in San Francisco, which evolved from an older system, is more elaborate and required heavier construction. In many respects, Los Angeles is building a high-speed suburban railroad, or electric interurban railway, instead of a light rail line. The cars will not have steps and load rapid transit-style with car floors at the same height as station platforms.

The line will begin in downtown Los Angeles in a joint subway station with RTD's heavy rail Metro line under Flower Street at Seventh Street. The light rail line will emerge from the subway near 12th and Flower streets and run in Flower Street and Washington Boulevard to the old Pacific Electric Railway right of way at about 20th Street and Long Beach Avenue West.

The line uses the former PE right of way for 16 miles to Willow Street in Long Beach, where it enters Long Beach Boulevard. A loop is planned on streets through downtown Long Beach.

Included in the project is relocation of the Southern Pacific (ex-PE) tracks used for freight service to make room for the passenger line. A freight-only bypass line will be built in Compton. There will be no joint passenger-freight tracks.

Five major grade separation projects are being built. In addition, the old PE Firestone Boulevard overpass and PE Los Angeles River Bridge are being replaced with new structures. There will be 33 at-grade crossings, all protected with warning devices and gates. The line will be equipped with cab signals similar to the San Francisco Muni Metro system. Twenty substations are planned to supply 750 volts DC to the overhead trolley wire. There will be 22 passenger stations.

Until the spring of 1988, the LACTC planned to construct the 16.5-mile Century Freeway line with light rail technology and ordered cars for both Long Beach and Century services. The Century line is now planned as an automated rail line, perhaps with rail cars similar to the light rail equipment, but more advanced. There has been talk of leasing surplus light rail cars to other systems.

Perhaps the most ironic aspect of the Long Beach project is that it follows over almost its entire length the Pacific Electric's Los Angeles-Long Beach electric interurban line opened on July 4, 1902, and abandoned by an RTD predecessor, the Los Angeles Metropolitan Transit Authority, on April 9, 1961. At one time the Pacific Electric, under Southern Pacific ownership, was the largest intercity electric railway in the world.

The estimated travel times for the light rail line will be similar to those on the old PE service. The light rail line's average speed, including station stops, is estimated to be 24.5 miles per hour. A Los Angeles-Long Beach trip will take 51.5 minutes, compared with 63 minutes on the express bus that replaced the PE in 1961.

WALDEMAR SIEVERS

The Los Angeles-Long Beach light rail line will follow exactly the offstreet right of way used by the Pacific Electric's Los Angeles-Long Beach interurban line from 1902 to 1961. The three-car Catalina steamer train, below, is approaching Vernon Avenue on Labor Day 1957, enroute to the dock near San Pedro. The light rail line will have a station at this same location. There were four tracks with the center pair for interurban trains and the outside ones for local cars and freight operation. The four-track section ended, above, at Watts, where the 103rd Street light rail station will be built. The picture, taken in 1945, shows a two-car train enroute to Los Angeles from Bellflower. The Pacific Electric was owned by Southern Pacific but couldn't survive the Southern California automobile culture. The SP abandoned most of the system, once the world's largest electric interurban railway, before selling the small remaining operation in 1953 to pro-bus investor Jesse Haugh, who abandoned the Glendale-Burbank and Hollywood lines in 1954-55 and sold the four remaining rail lines to a public transit authority in 1958.

HARRE W. DEMORO

With more than 1,200 streetcars in its heyday during the 1920s, the Los Angeles Railway Corp. was the largest rail transit system on the West Coast. The narrow-gauged yellow car system was developed by Henry Huntington, who also built the Pacific Electric but lost control of the Red Car interurban system to the SP in 1911. National City Lines bought the yellow system and renamed it Los Angeles Transit Lines in 1945. Although General Motors, Firestone Rubber, Phillips Petroleum, Mack Truck and Standard Oil of California had major stock holdings in NCL, the LATL bought 40 PCC streetcars and 130 trolley buses after World War II. By the time a public transit system took over in 1958, only the five PCC-equipped streetcar lines and two trolley bus lines were still electric, and these were converted in 1963. The car above is one of the hundreds of ''Huntington Standards'' the system operated between 1902 and 1952. Below, one of the streamlined PCC cars bought in 1937.

The Los Angeles County Transportation Commission has ordered 54 articulated, six-axle cars from Sumitomo Nippon/Sharyo for delivery starting in 1989. The 750-volt cars will have BBC chopper control and two BBC motors, and will be air conditioned and have air suspension. They are expected to weigh 94,000 pounds and have a 3 mph/sec. rate for acceleration and braking. Dynamic, air-applied disk brakes and magnetic track brakes will be used. The cars will not have steps and load only at platforms. They will have 56 seats. The car is to be 90 feet over couplers and 8' 9'' wide. With the decision to build the Century line with automated technology, there will be a surplus of light rail cars and there have been discussions about selling some of the cars. The map on the left shows the county's comprehensive transit master plan when the Century line was planned as a light rail route. On the page opposite are construction views, showing the roof being completed on the new light rail maintenance shop and workmen in the subway tunnel under Flower Street in downtown Los Angeles in 1988. The Los Angeles track gauge will be 4' 8½''.

COOKSEY/LACTC

The Los Angeles-Long Beach line is being built with welded rail attached to concrete ties with clips, as shown at left near North Long Beach in 1988. The ties are expected to last 50 years, 20 years longer than wooden ones. Workmen, below, are pouring concrete on the deck of the structure that will take the light rail cars into the yard and maintenance shop being built in the area bounded by the Long Beach Freeway, Los Angeles River, Carson Street and the rail line right of way. Three major buildings were under construction in 1988: a 3,700 square foot paint shop, a 30,000 square foot repair building and a 35,000 square foot structure with shop space and an operations center. The first cars are scheduled to arrive at the yard in March 1989 and the yards and shops are scheduled for completion in July 1989.

BOTH/LACTC

County Transit
WE'RE ON THE RIGHT TRACK
For more information, call the Guadalupe Corridor Public Information Office at (408) 971-6777.

ARTY
ARTY METRO

INSERT
738452
FEB 88
FAST PASS
$25
SAN FRANCISCO
MUNI
BART

Nº 000800
Guest Pass
San Diego Trolley
Issued by J. Seitner
Valid to 6/14
CENTRE CITY

San Diego Trolley
Timetable
CENTRE CITY
1009
San Diego Trolley Inc.
Effective February 6, 1983

Portland

San Diego

San Jose

Sacramento

San Jose

Predecessors

The designs of the San Jose and Portland light rail cars were based on rolling stock already introduced on other systems. San Jose's double-ended cars are similar to the new single-ended articulated streetcars, above, built by UTDC for Toronto, which have a trolley pole instead of a pantograph. The car, at Long Branch in March 1988, seats 61 passengers and is 77' 2'' long over couplers and 75' 1'' over body ends. Its maximum speed is 50 miles per hour, and the air conditioned car weighs about 80,900 pounds. The track gauge is 4' 10 7/8'' and the voltage 600. The Portland car evolved from the Rio de Janeiro pre-metro car, below, built by BN (formerly La Brugeoise Et Nivelles-Belgium). Eight of the cars were built completely by BN, and 60 more were manufactured in Brazil by Cobrasma Sumare' ''S.A.,'' under license. The car operates both on overhead trolley and electric third rail. It is 90' 7'' long over couplers, 82' 7'' over body ends, weighs 83,600 pounds and seats 58. The track gauge is 5' 3'' and the voltage 750. The car's maximum speed is 50 miles per hour.

Muni Metro signal tests at the Van Ness Avenue subway station in October 1979.

Bibliography

Books

Demoro, Harre W., *California's Electric Railways*, Interurban Press, Glendale, 1986..

Dodge, Richard V., *Rails of the Silver Gate*, Pacific Railway Journal, San Marino, 1960.

Forty, Ralph, *San Diego's South Bay Interurban*, Interurban Press, Glendale, 1987.

Hatcher, Colin K. and Tom Schwarzkopf, *Edmonton's Electric Transit*, Railfare, Toronto, 1983.

Hanft, Robert, *San Diego & Arizona, The Impossible Railroad*, Trans-Anglo Books, Glendale, 1984.

Kashin, Seymour and Harre W. Demoro, *An American Original, The PCC Car*, Interurban Press, Glendale, 1986.

Labbe, John T., *Fares Please! Those Portland Trolley Years*, Caxton, Caldwell, Idaho, 1980.

McCaleb, Charles, *Tracks, Tires, and Wires*, Interurban Press, Glendale, 1981.

McKane, John and Anthony Perles, *Inside Muni*, Interurban Press, Glendale, 1982.

Middleton, William D., *The Time of the Trolley*, Kalmbach, Milwaukee, 1967. Being reissued as three volumes by Golden West Books.

Mills, James R., *A Disorderly House, the Brown-Unruh Years in Sacramento*, Heyday Books, Berkeley, 1987.

O'Donnell, Terence and Thomas Vaughan, *Portland: an Informal History and Guide*, Oregon Historical Society, Portland, 1976, revised, 1984.

Partridge, Larry, *Mind the Doors, Please! The Story of Toronto and its Streetcars*, The Boston Mills Press, Erin, Ontario, 1983.

Perles, Anthony, with John McKane, Tom Matoff and Peter Straus, *The People's Railway*, Interurban Press, Glendale, 1981.

Statistical Abstract of the United States, 107th edition U.S. Department of Commerce, Bureau of the Census, Washington, D.C., December 1986.

California Cities, Towns & Counties, Edith R. Horner, ed., Hornwood Press, Palo Alto, 1987.

Transit in San Francisco: A Selected Chronology 1850-1987, Robert Callwell, ed., community affairs department, Municipal Railway of San Francisco, 1988.

Reports

Light Rail Vehicle Improvement Program for San Francisco Municipal Railway, two volumes, Louis T. Klauder & Associates, Philadelphia, April and May 1985.

The Composite Report, San Francisco Bay Area Rapid Transit District, May 1962.

Muni Metro Light Rail Operations, San Francisco Municipal Railway, undated, circa 1988.

Standard Light Rail Vehicle, by R.F. Muehlberger, Massachusetts Bay Transportation Authority, American Society of Mechanical Engineers, 73-ICT-80, June 5, 1973.

The Sixty-Mile Circle, Security Pacific Corp., Los Angeles, 1984.

Portland's Light Rail Project, Construction Completion of MAX, Ronald B. Higbee and Scott R. Farnsworth, paper presented to APTA Rail Conference, Toronto, June 16, 1987.

Light Rail-Banfield-I205, Tri-Met, Portland, no date.

Assessing the Performance of Portland's New LRVs, Dennis L. Porter, Tri-Met, presented to APTA Rail Conference, Toronto, June 16, 1987.

Urban Decision Making for Transportation Investments, Portland's Light Rail Transit System, Tri-County Metropolitan Transportation District of Oregon, Portland State University, distributed March 1985 by U.S. Department Transportation.

On and About MAX: Portland's Light Rail System, by Tom Matoff and Ken Zatarain, Tri-Met and Association of American Geographers, Portland, April 1987.

Light Rail Transit: Summary of Workshop Proceedings, Harre W. Demoro, ed., Santa Clara County Transportation Agency, April 23-25, 1979.

Light Rail Transit, A State of the Art Review, De Leuw, Cather & Co., U.S. Department of Transportation, DOT UT 50009, 1976.

Planning and Design of Vancouver's ALRT System, by Tom Parkinson, BC Rapid Transit Project, June 1985.

Articles

"Two Cars in Portland, Ore.," *Electric Railway Journal*, October 24, 1914, pp. 948-949.

"Transit Trauma," by Bill (Leon) Dorais, *San Francisco Magazine*, September 1967, pp. 32-35, 58-59.

"San Francisco's Muni Metro and Light Rail Transit System," by Rino Bei, *Light Rail Transit Planning*